Serving Latino Teens

Recent titles in
Libraries Unlimited Professional Guides for Young Adult Librarians
C. Allen Nichols and Mary Anne Nichols, Series Editors

The Guy-Friendly Teen Library: Serving Male Teens
Rollie Welch

Serving Urban Teens
Paula Brehm-Heeger

The Teen-Centered Writing Club: Bringing Teens and Words Together
Constance Hardesty

More Than MySpace: Teens, Librarians, and Social Networking
Robyn Lupa, Editor

Visual Media for Teens: Creating and Using a Teen-Centered Film Collection
Jane Halsall and R. William Edminster

Teen-Centered Library Service: Putting Youth Participation into Practice
Diane P. Tuccillo

Booktalking with Teens
Kristine Mahood

Make Room for Teens!: Reflections on Developing Teen Spaces in Libraries
Michael G. Farrelly

Teens, Libraries, and Social Networking: What Librarians Need to Know
Denise E. Agosto and June Abbas, Editors

Starting from Scratch: Building a Teen Library Program
Sarah Ludwig

Serving Teen Parents: From Literacy Skills to Life Skills
Ellin Klor and Sarah Lapin

Teens Go Green!: Tips, Techniques, Tools, and Themes in YA Programming
Valerie Colston

Serving Latino Teens

Salvador Avila

Libraries Unlimited Professional Guides for Young Adult Librarians
C. Allen Nichols and Mary Anne Nichols

AN IMPRINT OF ABC-CLIO, LLC
Santa Barbara, California • Denver, Colorado • Oxford, England

Library of Congress Cataloging-in-Publication Data

Avila, Salvador.
  Serving Latino teens / Salvador Avila.
    pages cm. — (Libraries Unlimited professional guides for young adult librarians series)
  Includes bibliographical references and index.
  ISBN 978-1-59884-609-6 (pbk.) — ISBN 978-1-59884-610-2 (ebook) (print)
 1. Hispanic Americans and libraries. 2. Young adults' libraries—United States.
 3. Libraries and teenagers—United States. I. Title.
 Z711.92.H56A955 2012
 027.62'6—dc23   2012013578

ISBN: 978-1-59884-609-6
EISBN: 978-1-59884-610-2

16 15 14 13 12   1 2 3 4 5

This book is also available on the World Wide Web as an eBook.
Visit www.abc-clio.com for details.

Libraries Unlimited
An Imprint of ABC-CLIO, LLC

ABC-CLIO, LLC
130 Cremona Drive, P.O. Box 1911
Santa Barbara, California 93116-1911

This book is printed on acid-free paper ∞
Manufactured in the United States of America

Contents

Series Foreword

Librarians have come to realize that understanding our teen patrons is vital to planning and services. We are better prepared to provide targeted programs and collections to meet unique characteristics of teens and reach certain demographics within our library communities. The Hispanic population in the United States has grown, especially in the last decade. We are very excited that Salvador Avila has written *Serving Latino Teens* as the newest addition to our series. Avila provides solid information that addresses the social and cultural characteristics of this teen demographic and offers strategies for serving them in the library.

We are proud of our association with Libraries Unlimited/ABC-CLIO, which continues to prove itself to be the premier publisher of books to help library staff serve teens. This series has succeeded because our authors know the needs of those library employees who work with young adults. Without exception, they have written useful and practical handbooks for library staff.

We hope you find this book, as well as our entire series, to be informative, providing you with valuable ideas as you serve teens, and that this work will further inspire you to do great things to make teens welcome in your library. If you have an idea for a title that could be added to our series, or would like to submit a book proposal, please e-mail us at lu-books@lu.com. We'd love to hear from you.

Mary Anne Nichols
C. Allen Nichols
Series Editors

Apá, we think of you every single day.

Special Thanks:

Barbara Ittner, Libraries Unlimited
&
Familia Avila

Introduction

Expanding capacity requires a willingness to endure short-term discomfort in the service of long-term reward.

—Jim Loehr and Tony Schwartz,
The Power of Full Engagement

The Need for This Book

In the Latino community, and among Latino teens in particular, pregnancy rates and school dropout rates are high, and college entrance percentages are low. Latino teens also face difficulties arising from immigration issues and the bilingual education controversy. This is relatively common knowledge. It is also no secret that teens experiencing such problems are unlikely to be library users. This book focuses on offering library services that center on awareness and prevention of these problems, provide encouragement, and foster leadership skills. Hopefully, this approach will "push the envelope," bringing innovative teen-centered library services.

What should not come as a surprise to you is the presence of Latino teens in your community. The population growth of Latino teens has been well documented and forecasted. For example, a 2000 *American Demographics* article observed that "between 2001 and 2010, the percentage of Hispanic children aged 5 to 9 will increase by 21 percent while the number of Hispanic 10- to 14-year-olds will increase by a whopping 29 percent" (Wellner 2000, 62).

Latinos bring much to the table, and their influence on our society is undeniable. *Hispanic/Latino Market Profile*, published by the Magazine Publishers of America (MPA) found in 2007 that "the Hispanic/Latino teen influence is evident in virtually every product category, from food to personal care to fashion" (MPA 2007, 11). And there are many more social, economic, psychological, technological, and sexual influences that might be discussed. However, let's focus on the political and educational impacts. Library Hotline reports that "Currently Hispanics account for more than 23 percent of kindergartners in private and public schools, according to 2007 data—more than three times the percentage of Hispanics in the 1970s. At the same time, more Hispanic kindergartners in 2007 were U.S.-born than foreign-born, assuring them of citizenship that will make them eligible to vote by 2020" (Hispanic enrollment 2009, 7).

In June of 2004 the National Endowment for the Arts (NEA) published *A Nation at Risk*, which took many by surprise. It stated that recreational reading was declining among all facets of society, especially among underrepresented groups. The fact that reading was losing ground hit librarians hard, and they became quite defensive. Unfortunately, things have not gotten much better. In a second NEA report titled *To Read or Not to Read: A Question of National Consequence*, Sunil Iyengar found that:

1. Young adults are reading fewer books in general;

2. Reading is declining as an activity among teenagers; and

3. Teens and young adults spend less time reading than people of other age groups (Iyengar 2007, 7, 8).

Most libraries claim to serve teens as a whole, and that tends to be true. But when we look at the specifics, and how they relate to library services to Latino teens, that assertion doesn't hold up. There is such great diversity among Latino teens that they should not be lumped into one group; therein lies the complexity of serving them. In subsequent chapters we will explore some of the multifaceted characteristics of Latino teens. The following are compelling points to ensure that teen services are not compromised nor excluded during turbulent economic times when eliminating services is common practice. There is also substantial scientific research that supports making Latino teens a prime target for library services. I may be stating the obvious, but libraries need to stop applying "traditional practices" that do not serve their constituents well and embrace what would benefit the community the most and bring a good long-term return on investment. Another challenge in serving Latino teens comes from within the profession in the form of turf wars, especially if a new service or initiative is involved.

Purpose and Scope of This Book

Serving Latino Teens aims to assist public and school librarians with most aspects of providing library services to teens of Latino heritage. This includes identifying the who, what, when, where, and whys of the Latino teen as it relates to his or her cultural, social, economic, psychological, technological, and sexual characteristics. If you are noticing an increase in teen library usage in general and a surge of Latino teen users specifically, this book will come in handy as a practical resource guide and clearinghouse of information that you can instantaneously implement. *Serving Latino Teens* not only stresses and aggressively advocates for services to Latino teens but also shows you how to best reach this demographic.

So, who are these Latino teens? They may be Spanish speakers, or they may be bilingual or English speakers. They may be recent immigrants—or New Americans—or they may be second or third generation. They may be poor or rich; dark skinned or pale white; play sports (not just soccer) or be part of a choir; and so forth. In short, they are unique individuals with multiple characteristics and interests and should be considered first as such.

This guide goes beyond the general concepts of serving teens and the need to serve Latino teens in particular. You will actually read how to *best* serve them. Grounded in empirical evidence, this book presents what the scientific community says is important to teens and shows how to incorporate this information into your services.

You will not just read about the need for a relevant collection. You will discover books, series, and magazines being read by Latino teens. You will not just read about new skills to serve teens. You will find out which actual skills are needed to offer relevant and responsive library services to Latino teens. The generalities of serving teen library patrons transcend ethnicities, but reaching Latino teens requires linking these general services to their specific needs. *Reaching Out to Religious Youth* contends that "Buddhist teens want what most teens want—to be valued, accepted as part of their community and to find their place in the world. They examine their parents' and communities' values, and then determine which are most important to them individually. They seek to assert their individuality while maintaining their place in their extended family" (Carman 2004, 192). So it is with Latino teens.

Much painstaking time has been spent compiling this information so that you do not get caught up in doing extensive research. In other words, this book can save you precious time and energy that could be better spent in creating public value.

What Is Not Covered?

Serving Latino Teens does not address general issues that have already been covered in print. For example, if you are interested in serving urban youth or male teens or handling social networking or digital issues, these are covered in the Libraries Unlimited Professional Guides for Young Adult Librarians series. *Serving Latino Teens* picks up where this great series left off by offering additional in-depth information, research, and tailored library services targeting Latino teens.

Latino teens basically share the needs and wants of general population non-Latino teens, yet they are also cognizant that they are different to some degree. We need to be aware of these characteristics, whether they are cultural, social, economic, psychological, technological, sexual, and so forth.

A Few Words about Terminology

In this guide, teens are referred to as customers. There is a continuous discourse regarding what term we should employ to describe our users. To a great extent it has not been agreed upon on what the proper and/or appropriate term is. I offer this justification for using "customer." Other professions have their respective terms for their users. For example, in the airport community, users are referred to as souls. Doctors refer to them as patients. Lawyers refer to them as clients. Libraries offer many services. Traditionally, they are best known for loaning materials. Therefore, the word "patron" best represented them. But times are different now. In addition to loaning materials, libraries are in the commons, community center–based institutions, and programming business. It seems as if library users are now making use of more services than just checking out materials, and therefore I now consider them customers more so than patrons. Another point of contention surrounding terminology is what word should be used to refer to our targeted segment of the community. Should we use Hispanic, Latino, Hispanic American, Colombian, or what? The answer is "it all depends." First, who are you asking to answer the question: adults or teens? You will receive contrasting responses from different people. These individuals will generally respond in a way that is partially biased, in that they will advance the terminology that best suits their needs. A 2009 article titled "Are You Hispanic?" asked which term was preferable, "Hispanic" or "Latino." "Hispanic" was preferred by 36 percent, while 21 percent preferred "Latino." Forty-three percent had no preference (Simeone 2009, 26).

At the same time the companion book to the CNN series *Latino in America* says this about "Latino": "Latino is an American identity. It is a word to describe Americans who are drawn to each other by this intangible cultural link, the similarity of the way we run our families, our devotion to faith, and the warmth of our personalities, our connection to a people who celebrate the new culture they've created in the United States while struggling each day with whether we need to assimilate or integrate into this new society" (O'Brien 2009, 5). The author then elaborates on this term: "This young population wants to identify as Latino, they want to speak the Spanish of their ancestors no matter how many generations they are removed from immigration. They are proud of who they are, just as I am" (O'Brien 2009, 6).

The mayor of Los Angeles has gone on record as saying that he is an American of Latino descent. Today's Latino teens have the same pressure of labeling as previous generations. This indicates that things have not changed in the Latino community. For example, recent immigrants, both adults and teens, for the most part associate themselves with their country of origin. Second-generation teens are now U.S. citizens who have ties with both countries and remain bilingual to a certain degree. Third-generation teens tend to be fully assimilated individuals who are aware of their cultural backgrounds but don't necessarily display them. They understand that they are Latino but also realize that they are U.S. citizens first. They might entertain the notion of traveling to their parents' native countries, but have no intentions of permanently moving back. Their life is here! I have observed and personally polled young adults about their feelings about returning to their native countries to pursue a life there. Hands down, the majority of the young adults have absolutely no desire to return. The reasons are plentiful and range from no future to culture clash to no opportunities. This is what Rick Sanchez, host of CNN's "Rick's List," has to say about the subject of assimilation:

> Much of what many Americans say about Mexicans and other Hispanics, describing them as intruders and outsiders, is no different than what was said in the past about the Germans, the Irish, the Italians, the Jews, the Poles, the Swedes, and the Norwegians, just to name a few. It's a part of our history. And experts say that history has proven again and again that immigrant groups assimilate as English-speaking Americans within two generations. And they say it's happening now again. (Sanchez 2010, 229)

For the purposes of this book, the term "Latinos" has been selected as the preferred terminology. First and foremost, it encompasses all groups into one term. It is also a self-applied term that is generally accepted by the majority of ethnicities; is politically neutral; is embraced and for the most part used by think tanks that focus on Latino research and issues; and more accurately portrays the lifestyle under one umbrella term. Furthermore, the few other books that exist on library services to this segment of the population use "Latino." You will always find individuals who oppose this term or elect to use others, but for the sake of this conversation, "Latino" is victorious over other terms.

Where Libraries Fit In

June Garcia and Susan Kent say that "a library cannot and should not fill every possible role. However, a new vision for any library system should incorporate new roles, new technologies, new collections, and new or renovated facilities to enable it to meet community needs for the present and the future" (Garcia and Kent 2009, 2). Many librarians, especially teen librarians, believe that the time to act is now (or even overdue): Latino teens should be identified as an emerging service priority. Latino teens—as well as teens in general—can no longer be an afterthought when it comes to providing library services.

How does all of this terminology and demographic information relate to librarianship? Libraries are ideal places for all teens to complete their homework, socialize with friends, volunteer, and learn something that is of interest to them. This book asserts that Latino teens have more similarities with non-Latino teens than differences. Therefore, it is imperative that libraries act as influential stakeholders and trendsetters in these peoples' lives, whether it is in a physical building or online.

Roy Oldenburg talks about "the third place." According to Oldenburg, "third places that render the best and fullest service are those to which one may go alone at almost any time of the day or evening with assurance that acquaintances will be there. To have such a place available whenever the demons of loneliness or boredom strike or when the pressures and frustrations of the day call for relaxation amid good company is a powerful resource" (Oldenburg 1999, 32). The amazing thing is that libraries are perfect third places.

Most Latino teens are well aware of their impact on society and astute as to their positions and roles. Many Latino teens are defined by surroundings and popular culture and not necessarily by language. For example, when discussing preferred terminology, it would be wrong to assume that they all will favor one term over another. When asked about cultural identity, many of today's Latino teens might respond with "I'm Cuban" or "I'm Colombian." This is due to the fact that the Latino community is so diverse that other people do not know if they are actually Cuban, Mexican, Puerto Rican, or from one of the many other Latino countries. In addition, the parents of these teens have often instilled pride in their country of origin or heritage culture, and as a result, they will respond accordingly The media, in tandem with these two forces, are elevating the teens' awareness of their identities, promoting on your television screen everything from lowriders to name brands using Latino celebrities, such as Lugz using Cain Velasquez, current Ultimate Fighting Championship (UFC) Heavyweight Champion, to promote their products. George Lopez and other prominent celebrities are also making Latino culture more noticeable and appealing. Latino teens are confident and proud to be who they are. Some general statistics about Latino teens:

- In 2020, the Hispanic/Latino teen market will balloon 62% larger than today—growing six times faster than the rest of the teen market; and

- Today, Hispanic/Latino teens are 4.6 million strong—representing 20% of all U.S. teenagers (*Market Profile* 2004, 11).

During the process of writing this book, I noticed headlines in many library publications: "Santa Cruz Library Board Delays Decision on Cuts," "Cincinnati PL Faces Painful Drop in State Fund," and "Proposed CT Budget Slashes Library Aid"; and that's just a few. In fact, most libraries are experiencing extensive budget shortfalls. This means that services of some sort are going to be eliminated. The question now becomes which services, collections, and staffing will be eliminated. Being a teen advocate means that one is going to do everything humanly possible to restore library funding and either continue and/or commence serving teens.

Currently many research companies are making groundbreaking studies in the area of Latino demographics. Much of this research is compiled, shared, and cited throughout this book. Librarians only need to find it, read it, familiarize themselves with it, understand it, and use it in their practices. This knowledge allows you to master your domain.

In recent years, the Latino community is the one group that has made the greatest population gain in this country and has been receiving a great deal of attention. Rightfully so, as they are changing the demographic composition of this country. This demographic shift is causing many complications for almost every public agency, including libraries. For example, just a few years ago it was commonly held that the majority of Latinos were first generation. The most recent Census Bureau information reveals that the majority of Latinos are U.S. born. Knowing who your Latino teens are requires careful diagnosis. Why? Because you still have Latino teens with widely varied backgrounds. A great deal of empirical evidence confirms that serving teens is indeed the beginning of a new service point in libraryland. One way of measuring our success could be to find out the reading competencies of the patrons we serve or to see if school reading levels also indicate an increase in reading skills. According to the *Nation's Report Card: Reading 2007*, the future looks promising as reading scores have progressed over the years. Hispanic students scored higher in 2007 than they did in the years 1992 and 2005, respectively. For the most part, Hispanic students' scores were higher in both years and grade levels that were monitored.

Why We Should Serve Latino Teens

With this in mind, *Serving Latino Teens* focuses on sharing similarities among and differences between Latino teens and non-Latino teens. How do these similarities and differences apply to librarianship, and how can we turn Latino teens into productive and intelligent members of society, all while using the library?

One of the most important reasons why we should be serving teens, including Latino teens, comes from the American Library Association (ALA). *The State of America's Libraries* explains that "adolescents comprise a significant proportion of the American population, and many of them are library users" (ALA 2010, 10).

You may notice that many of the ideas, approaches, and recommendations in this book run contrary to traditional and current practices. These new guidelines emphasize the importance of culture over language usage, particularly the preference for English among all factions of the Latino community, especially teens. Conversely, as stressed in *Crash Course in Serving Spanish Speakers* (Avila 2008), this is not to be confused with a one size fits all approach. There is a time and place where the use of culture is more critical than the usage of language. At this particular point in time, it is still not fully known whether Latino teens prefer culture over language or language over culture. After reviewing all contributing factors on this subject, it is my hunch that language is or will soon supersede the culture component in importance. Although language is a subset of culture, by focusing on culture, we also include cultural characteristics, heritage, traditions, values, and belief systems of Latino teens. We tout services to Latino teens, but our efforts haven't come to full fruition yet. Slowly and surely they are getting their due respect. The great news is that librarians generally understand the paradigm of this growth and are recognizing the importance of Latino teens by attending training sessions, reallocating resources, or reading books on the subject.

Each chapter in this book represents a step in the evolution of rendering library services to teens, which also happens to highlight best practices and relevant and responsive services and programs and reframes our approach to serving this segment of the population. After reading the entire book you will be able to proudly and expertly speak to the library needs of Latino teens. However, keep in mind that there is also a constant, ever-evolving educational process that comes along with working with teens, and in particular, Latino teens.

Another ambition of *Serving Latino Teens* is thus to create a practical and effective understanding of Latino teens; we librarians need to be constantly updating our perceptions of what is relevant and responsive. There are many great practices we employ when serving teens. While some of these practices come and go in library services, *Serving Latino Teens* offers the foundation of an applicable and receptive approach.

As previously stated, the goal of this book is to help library staff identify opportunities to improve their services to this emerging and expanding segment of our community. Latino teens can be tremendous assets to society, and libraries are well positioned to support their educational and recreational library needs. *Serving Latino Teens* presents a composite of best practices as well as policies and cultural information that support a better understanding of their unique attributes.

The book is unique for several reasons: it gathers together in one place information on the topic; offers transferable skills and talent that may be easily duplicated; is the most complete and up-to-date discussion of the subject in library community; and is the only one to specifically address serving Latino teens. With the Latino teen segment of the community being so diverse and with so many best practices available on serving them, you might wonder which approach is right for you and your library system. In this book you'll find the best information and approaches to date.

Enjoy your journey!

References

American Library Association. 2010. *The State of America's Libraries*. http:// www.ala.org/news/sites/ala.org.news/files/content/mediapresscenter/ americaslibraries/soal2010/ALA_Report_2010-ATI001-NEW1.pdf [accessed March 26, 2012].

Avila, Salvador. 2008. Crash Course in Serving Spanish Speakers. Westport, CT: Libraries Unlimited.

Carman, Kay. 2004. *Reaching out to religious youth*. Westport, CT: Libraries Unlimited.

Garcia, June, and Susan Kent. 2009. The challenge of change. Report to the Mayor's Task Force on the Revitalization and Future of the Chattanooga-Hamilton County Bicentennial Library. http://www.chattanooga.gov/Files/CHCBL_Report_FINAL_02_16_09.pdf [accessed March 13, 2012].

Hispanic enrollment in schools is rising. 2009. *Library Hotline* 38, no. 10 (March 16).

Iyengar, Sunil. 2007. *To read or not to read: a question of national consequence*. Washington, D.C.: National Endowment for the Arts.

Lee, J., W. Grigg, and P. Donahue. 2007. *The nation's report card: Reading 2007* (NCES 2007-496). Washington, D.C.: National Center for Education Statistics, Institute of Education Sciences, U.S. Department of Education.

Loehr, Jim, and Tony Schwartz. 2003. *The power of full engagement*. New York: Free Press.

Magazine Publishers of America. 2007. *Hispanic/Latino market profile*. www.magazine.org/marketprofiles [accessed March 13, 2012].

O'Brien, Soledad. 2009. *Latino in America*. New York: Penguin.

Oldenburg, Ray. 1999. *The great good place*. New York: Marlowe & Company.

Sanchez, Rick. 2010. *Conventional idiocy: Why the new America is sick of old politics*. New York: Penguin.

Simeone, Stacey. 2009. Are you Hispanic? *Poder Enterprises Magazine* 68 (October).

Wellner, Alison Stein. 2000. Generation Z. *American Demographics* 22.9: 61–65.

1

Who are Latino Teens?

Teens (12- to 19- year-olds), in general, are sought after as the ultimate consumers and creators of trends. The Hispanic teen segment may be one of the most important markets for future-oriented marketers to understand.

—Magazine Publishers of America,
Hispanic/Latino Market Profile

Diversity does not even begin to define the Latino teen state of being. Their cultural, social, economical, psychological, technological, and sexual predilections are endless. Furthermore, "one in five teens in the U.S. is Hispanic and they are growing six times faster than other market segments. By 2020, they will account for 24% of the population aged five to 19 years," according to *Nuestro Futuro: Hispanic Teens in Their Own Words*. This provides an important reason why we should continue to serve Latino teens.

Geraldo Rivera, one of the most recognized Latino news correspondents and producer and host of several of his own shows, asserts that "by 2030, one in five Americans will be Hispanic, according to U.S.

Census Bureau projections. If you are talking about American teenagers, then as of 2009 one in five teens is Hispanic already" (Rivera 2009, 67).

Characteristics of Latino Teens

You may consider serving Latino teens to be the same as serving the general teen population. However, Latino teens within Generation Y or Generation Z are often bilingual and bicultural and have varied cultural, social, economical, psychological, technological, and sexual characteristics. These unique conditions present librarians with several challenges. Consequently, to best serve Latino teens, your first step is to pinpoint those features that are the most outstanding within your teen community; that will subsequently determine which approach you embark on.

The current magnitude and undoubted potential growth that exist within the Latino teen community are a true opportunity to create public value. Furthermore, serving Latino teens should not be seen as a passive activity; to the contrary, there should be profound and proactive support from administration regarding the benefits. Kit Yarrow and Jayne O'Donnell, authors of *Gen BuY: How Tweens, Teens and Twenty-Something Are Revolutionizing Retail*, avow that "generation Y, those born between 1978 and 2000, has overtaken baby boomers in sheer numbers and is poised to do the same with its income by 2017" (Yarrow and O'Donnell 2009, xi).

Without typecasting Latino teens, we need to know where Latino teens rank among these statistics. In general, Latino teens should be showing precursors to better reading habits as they become more proficient in English, stay in school longer, and look forward to a prosperous and bright future. The fact that they are not reading orthodox textbooks or books from reading lists does not necessarily imply that they do not read. Consider this statement to commence discussing who Latino teens are: Latino teens are not as interested in Latino staff or Spanish-language books as much as librarians who are sensitive to their needs and wants. Does this come as a surprise? Richard Fry and Jeffrey S. Passel's *Latino Children: A Majority Are U.S.-Born Offspring of Immigrants* is a snapshot of the current state of Latino teens by generation. One of the most revealing facts about languages pertaining to Latino children ages five and older is that the higher the generation the more likely that English will be spoken, whereas, first- and second-generation children will be Spanish dominant or bilingual. The study was published by the Pew Hispanic Center, one of the most well-known, respected, and authoritative think tanks, which delivers detailed research on Latino issues.

These statistics illustrate that teens with one foreign-born parent have the potential to be reared differently from teens with no foreign-born parents. Consider the dynamics of two households. Household A has two foreign-born parents, while Household B has one foreign-born parent. Let's assume that the second parent in Household B is a second-generation persona. We can infer that Household A has parents that may not be all that familiar with how their local government, school, library, and political processes work. This puts the Latino teen of this household at a disadvantage as the parents do not know how to mentor and/or protect their rights. Household B has one parent who has probably completed high school or has been in the States for quite some time and is more familiar with the expectations of raising an American family. They may be more prone to encourage their children to do their homework, assist with some translations where needed, and become more informed about resources that are readily available to them. One revealing example of how the tide is shifting in libraries' favor is that these emerging families think more highly of libraries than previous generations have. "U.S. 14- to 24-year-olds [of Latino heritage] were more likely to anticipate increased library use in the next three to five years than other U.S. age demographics. Forty-one percent of U.S. 14- to 17-year-olds and 31 percent of U.S. 18- to 24-year-olds anticipate increasing their use of the library" (De Rosa 2005, 1-5), according to a publication titled *Perceptions of Libraries and Information Resources*.

Speaking and Cultural Aptitude Types

Some Latino teens adapt to North American culture quickly while others do not. Some know about their cultural backgrounds (such as origins of parent and grandparents, basic knowledge of their histories), and others do not. For example, you notice many teens wearing shirts depicting Emiliano Zapata, but if you were to ask one to name a contribution of Zapata, they would not be able to do so. At this point, you know that they have pride in their culture and possibly need more outreach. When reaching out is done correctly you will notice a considerably different customer base. Take into account that when it comes to Latino teens, there are three main types of speaking aptitude skills: English dominant, bilingual, and Spanish dominant. Historically, scientific research has not fully elaborated on what type of Latino teens are being researched. However, the news for libraries looks bright. One of the most recent accounts asserts that "fifty-four percent of the Latino population visited libraries in the past year and that Latinos hold positive perceptions of libraries" (Flores and Pachon 2008, introduction). In the past, the parents of Latino teens have been more willing than the general population to increase their taxes to continue using library services. Don't they deserve our support?

Generation Ñ

To dig deeper into this subject, let's see what one of the premier marketers has to say about this Latino age group. M. Isabel Valdés, author of *Hispanic Customers for Life* describes this vibrant cohort as Generation Ñ. This Generation Ñ is the most written about segment of the Latino subgroups and has more than six million people. They take advantage of both worlds and have popular venues by which they become informed and mobilize themselves. Libraries should also focus on Latino teens because:

> This segment is presently leading the growth in the under age 18 category in the United States. While the non-Hispanic youth growth rate continues to decline, the Latino segment has grown exponentially. One in five teens in the United Sates is of Hispanic descent. Between 2005 and 2020 the Latino teen population is expected to grow 35.6 percent, compared with a decline of 2.6 percent among non-Hispanic whites. (Valdés 2008, 145)

Valdés is one of the most noteworthy Latino marketing gurus, and her book entertains and introduces many great practices that librarians may capitalize on.

Let's look at a different set of statistics. In 2009, Telemundo and Meredith Hispanic Ventures set out to find out what Latinas wanted out of life. Two of the major findings were:

1. Latinas are inspired by prior generations of women into action, empowerment, and self-development. Latinas have redefined their priorities and higher education and careers trump getting married.

2. Several results provided further proof that Latinas are enthusiastic about new technologies. Latinas are more likely than their non-Latina counterparts to use technological devices such as cell phones, digital cameras, and iPods.

The above information is a break from the past. In previous generations it was very common for Latino teens, both male and female, to watch Spanish-language soap operas or evening shows as a family activity. I make this observation from personal experience. Shared viewing of Spanish-language programs transcends today's families' nightly activities and also differs from what Latino teens report doing if the household has a tight bond. Oftentimes, watching Spanish-language television is much more prevalent in first-generation families, as the nearby aunt or other relatives might come over and have their nightly dosage of soap operas. Such is not the case with this new generation of teens. Depending on their level of acculturation, they are more likely to be on a computer or hanging out with friends.

In addition, in previous generations, parents brought their children up in a very traditional manner. Teens would come home right after school, look after younger family members, and have dinner together with the family. Once again, such is not the case nowadays. In many of today's households that don't practice the same traditional rituals as previous generations, today's Latino teens, like their non-Latino counterparts, might have after school extracurricular activities, be happily employed, and socialize away from home. There are competing things for Latino teens to do with their time, and librarians need to work hard to demonstrate the library's value so that Latino teens include them in their daily life. The question at this point is, how do libraries capitalize on these cultural and societal shifts? You'll find recommendations for specific programs later in this book (see appendix A).

Another awe-inspiring report that delves into the nature of today's Latino teens, *Nuestro Futuro: Hispanic Teens in Their Own Words*, was published in 2006. It reveals much that will be of interest to the library community and will help library staff better understand Latino teens. Researchers discovered that groups carry in-depth implications and that there were four characteristics common to many of their subjects:

1. Hispanic Teens are Teens First

2. Hispanic Teens are Complex

3. Hispanic Teens are Influential

4. Hispanic Teens are Optimistic

However, these identifiers are not "one-size-fits-all," and therein lies the challenge and beauty of diversity among Latino Teens. If you happen to read this report, you will find more detailed information that illustrates common threads about these four characteristics. Understanding and knowing these inclinations will help libraries render the right services, programs, collections, training sessions, and initiatives.

This is just the tip of the iceberg of understanding who Latino teens are. Raising your awareness of Latino teens' cultural, social, economical, psychological, technological, and sexual characteristics is beneficial even though it requires more work on your behalf. However, keep in mind that a good portion of library nonusers will remain nonusers, and Latino teens are not excluded from this fact. The expression that you have to walk in another's persons shoes to truly understand them could not be more appropriate with Latino teens. As working adults we have our own ideas of what it is that teens need to be able to be productive members of society. Even though this may be the best practice, it's wise to be cautious. That is why building a teen service point requires a philosophy of "by teens for teens," and that is why building a teen-centered team is important.

Carefully examine your services, collections, resources, and staffing. These all factor into how well you will serve your customers. Even though your services, collections, and resources are your bread and butter, a well-rounded staffing module has to be in place to ensure that your target audience is receptive to you and the library. For the most part, libraries have to create teen services with the existing staff or hire teen-centered staff after tenured staff members have left the profession. If you have staff that are nowhere near retirement and are going to be part of the teen services team, be sure to build their awareness and abilities before they interact with teens.

Staff Perceptions

Nurture and educate your staff so that they completely understand the task of serving teens. Find out what motivates staff and find strategies that will improve performance with existing motivators. If they happily agree to serve teens, and in particular teens of Latino heritage, you are in good shape. If a staff member is hesitant or not sure, you may want to rethink the placement.

For a prime example of a real life account that occurred in Colorado consider this personal narrative for what it means to be a Latina teen, *Just like Us: The True Story of Four Mexican Girls Coming of Age in America* (Thorpe 2009). Look beyond numbers, projections, and statistics and try to understand the journeys and experiences that Latino teens go through on a daily basis. Here's a description from the inside book jacket: "A powerful and moving account of four young women from Mexico who have lived most of their lives in the United States and attend the same high school. Two of them have legal documentation and two do not. *Just Like Us* is their story." The girls go through positive and negative experiences and occurrences common to Latino teens. All four end up attending college under different circumstances. What happens to them during and after college, and what happens to their families? One episode that may resonate with librarians reads: "Then one weekend she went to the public library and logged onto the Internet and discovered her grades: In her first quarter, she had received three A's and one B plus." One of the main characters knew that she could go to her local public library for Internet access.

On June 18, 2010, Latino USA (http://lantinousa.kut.org) featured "American Dreamer: Sam's Story." It is a story of a kid from Indiana who aspires to go to college, but there is one problem—he is not a U.S. citizen. His story may change your mind and perception of Latino teens. Not all Latino teens have this hardship, but there is no doubt that Sam will touch you with his poignant childhood and rearing and adulthood forecast. This story documents and captures the moving experience of just one Latino teen. There are many others.

U.S.-Born versus New Americans

U.S.-born Latino teens and New American teens may talk to each other, but tensions exist between the two groups. This type of division is easy to notice but sometimes hard to explain, and you may draw several conclusions as to why this is the case. U.S.-born Latino teens may see themselves as superior. New Latino American teens might not be accepted because of their limited English proficiency and understanding of new social norms and customs. Some teens are caught in the middle. One way to identify where Latino teens best fit in is by studying their cohorts, what classes they have been assigned to, what language they use the most, and the subject matter they are discussing. New American teens are most often found in English as a Second Language (ESL) classes and often form a bond with their classmates. U.S.-born Latino teens will have completely different competency levels and subjects and a variety of crowds to select from. You may see them as Latino teens with the same culture, but a cultural gap partitions the two types.

Some say the fatalism of Latin American cultures is a poor fit in a society built on Anglo-Saxon values. Over the course of several generations, the immigrant family typically loosens its identification with the old country and binds with the new. Depending on their generation, parents for the most part understand why teens need digital gear. Issues surface when parents don't agree with teens' lifestyle choices. How they dress. How they act. Why they spend so much time using these electronic gadgets, and so forth. Often, the parents and relatives of Latino teens belong to an exploited workforce, such as janitors, irrigators, workers in poultry plants, etc. A good read on the latter subject is *Catching Out: The Secret World of Day Laborers* (Reavis 2010), which offers a glimpse of what some parents and relatives might go through that could prevent a Latino teen from using your library services—no matter how relevant they are.

Even though generations, acculturation, parenting, and other contributing factors play a role in a Latino teen's success, where the teen lives should also be taken into consideration when rendering library services. In the *Tipping Point*, Malcolm Gladwell asserts that "peer pressure and community influence are more important than family influence in determining how children turn out. Studies of juvenile delinquency and high school dropout rates, for example, demonstrate that a child is better off in a good neighborhood and a troubled family than he or she is in a troubled neighborhood and a good family" (Gladwell 2000, 167).

One of the most recent studies to document what is important to Latino teens is *Between Two Worlds: How Young Latinos Come of Age in America*. A summary of the report's end results follows:

- Only in the third and higher generations do a majority of Hispanic youths (50 percent) use "American" as their first term of self-description;

- Hispanics are the largest and youngest minority group in the United States;

- Two-thirds of Hispanics ages 16 to 25 are native-born Americans. That figure may surprise those who think of Latinos mainly as immigrants. But the four-decades-old Hispanic immigration wave is now mature enough to have spawned a big second generation of U.S.-born children who are on the cusp of adulthood. Back in 1995, nearly half of all Latinos ages 16 to 25 were immigrants. This year marks the first time that a plurality (37 percent) of Latinos in this age group are the U.S.-born children of immigrants. An additional 29 percent are of third and higher generations. Just 34 percent are immigrants themselves;

- Latinos make up about 18 percent of all youth ages 16 to 25 in the United States.

- Asked which term they generally use first to describe themselves, young Hispanics show a strong preference for their family's country of origin (52 percent) over American (24 percent) or the terms "Hispanic" or "Latino" (20 percent) to identify themselves. Among the U.S.-born children of immigrants, the share that identifies first as American rises to one in three, and among the third and higher generations, it rises to half;

- By a ratio of about two to one, young Hispanics say there are more cultural differences (64 percent) than commonalities (33 percent) within the Hispanic community in the United States;

- Native-born Latino youths have a somewhat more negative view of teen parenthood than do the foreign born;

- The reason most often given by Latino youth who cut off their education before college is financial pressure to support a family. Nearly three-quarters of this group say this is a big reason for not continuing in school. About half cite poor English skills; about four in ten cite a dislike of school or a belief that they do not need more education for the careers they plan to pursue;

- About three in ten (31 percent) young Latinos say they have a friend or relative who is a current or former gang member. This degree of familiarity with gangs is much more prevalent among the native born than the foreign born—40 percent versus 17 percent.

As you can see, there is enough research from authoritative sources as to why libraries should focus on teens and include Latino teens in this quest. The journey may not be an easy one, but it is certainly one worth embarking on.

References

"American Dreamer: Sam's Story." June 23, 2010. Produced by Long Haul Productions. http://www.latinousa.org/2010/06/23/american-dreamer-sams-story/ Accessed on April 9, 2012.

Cisneros, Henry G., ed. 2008. *Latinos and the nation's future*. Houston: Arte Publico Press.

De Rosa, Cathy. 2005. *Perceptions of libraries and information resources*. Dublin, OH: OCLC.

Flores, Edward, and Harry Pachon. 2008. *Latinos and public library perceptions*. California: Tomas Rivera Policy Institute.

Fry, Richard, and Jeffrey S. Passel. 2008. *Latino children: A majority are U.S.-Born offspring of immigrants*. Washington, D.C.: Pew Hispanic Center.

Gladwell, Malcolm. 2000. *The tipping point.* New York: Little, Brown.

Magazine Publishers of America. 2004. *Hispanic/Latino market profile.* www.magazine.org/marketprofiles [accessed March 14, 2012].

Nuestro futuro: Hispanic teens in their own words. 2006. Redwood Shores, CA: Cheskin.

Pew Hispanic Center. 2009. *Between two worlds: How young Latinos come of age in America.* Washington, D.C.: Pew Hispanic Center.

Reavis, Dick J. 2010. *Catching out: The secret world of day laborers.* New York: Simon & Schuster.

Rivera, Geraldo. 2009. *The great progression: How Hispanics will lead America to a new era of prosperity.* New York: Penguin.

Thorpe, Helen. 2009. *Just like us: The true story of four Mexican girls coming of age in America.* New York: Scribner.

Valdés, M. Isabel. 2008. *Hispanic customers for life: A fresh look at acculturation.* New York: Paramount Market Publishing, Inc.

Yarrow, Kit, Ph.D., and Jayne O'Donnell. 2009. *Gen buY: How tweens, teens, and twenty-somethings are revolutionizing retail.* San Francisco: Jossey-Bass.

2

Issues

A library cannot and should not fill every possible role. However, a new vision for any library system should incorporate new roles, new technologies, new collections, and new or renovated facilities to enable it to meet community needs for the present and the future.

—June Garcia and Susan Kent, *The Challenge of Change. Report to the Mayor's Task Force on the Revitalization and Future of the Chattanooga-Hamilton County Bicentennial Library*

When discussing issues affecting today's Latino teens, it is particularly interesting to examine the discourse on why Latino teens either participate in or are subject to any of the many varieties of nonacceptable social ills. Some of these ills, which we will examine shortly, are teen pregnancy, gangs and criminal behavior, dropout rates, low educational achievements, hate crime, and lack of parental guidance.

Teens from all walks of life may, inadvertently or advertently, fall into pitfalls created by current circumstances. These teens' mishaps require immediate attention and solutions. Once we know why Latino teens do what they do, we will be better prepared to understand, approach, and offer supportive, motivational, and practical advice—perhaps even some counseling. Understanding the root of social tribulations can help decelerate or even reverse their impact on today's youth. By focusing on the core issues, instead of just placing bandages over these serious matters, we are empowered to help.

Six Social Issues

Some of the issues of great concern to our communities in relation to Latino teens as well as other teens include, but are not limited to pregnancy, drugs, criminal activities, and dropout/vagrancy. Even though dealing with these problems does not fall within the library's traditional scope of services and programs, it is worth paying some attention to these sticky situations. If you think the current teen scenario is scary, consider the future of teens if libraries and other agencies do not tackle these issues. There is simply too much to lose if we do not take into account or pay no attention to the social issues that affect today's Latino teens.

This chapter introduces you to these social issues that affect Latino teens, helps you comprehend their seriousness, and finally shows what libraries can do to alleviate the predicament.

As we already know, teens are a moving target. They have minds of their own. They feel they are invincible—depending on their age. Yet, they are still humans who could do with a place that fosters and nurtures a sense of belonging. What better place than the local public library? Before getting too far in our discussion, consider these two questions.

- What are your aspirations for helping teens with these issues; or, what actual attainment benchmark would you be happy with?

- Is an ounce of prevention or person-to-person activity good enough; or can you create more public value by decreasing bad statistics and increasing good statistics?

Six issues currently plaguing Latino teens rank among the most troubling and will be briefly discussed in this chapter. They are, in no order of priority:

- Teen pregnancy;

- Gangs and criminal behavior;

- Dropout rates;

- Low educational achievements;

- Hate crime; and

- Lack of parental guidance.

Libraries are generally geared toward literacy needs and providing services that take place inside the physical library. Many staff are unwilling to look beyond these services. Serving Latino teens is more than a set of tasks; it's a transformation of library services and your role as a librarian. The issues discussed here are not simple in scope, and dealing with them requires skills and talents beyond the library's capacity. But where there are challenges, there are also opportunities. With today's library resources, employed and implemented properly, you are in a prime position to make a difference. Let's take a closer look at the six issues above, assess their negative impacts, and see how libraries may be of assistance.

Teen Pregnancy

The National Hispanic Medical Association (NHMA) issued a report in the spring of 2009 that stated that "Hispanics face severe lack of access to health care, lack of trust and knowledge, and are low-income, poorly educated with strong cultural and family values, limited English proficiency, mainly living in urban areas" (NHMA 2009). This should come as no surprise, as the media have definitely broadcasted to the entire country information about the health issues among the Latino community. The irony is that the entire country does not have a health strategy in mind. The fitness and well-being of Latino youth are at risk every single day for our lack of a vested interest in their physical condition. Among Latino teens, the by-products of this lack of commitment to health are obvious. One of the most damaging and urgent issues with Latina teens is pregnancy. Compounding the issue is the absence of male responsibility and involvement.

There is no lack of literature, initiatives, research, and recommendations on Latina pregnancy. To better understand the expecting and pregnant Latina teen, consider the most recent scientific research pertaining to this subject. Working in collaboration the National Women's Law Center and the Mexican American Legal Defense and Education Fund have succinctly documented Latina issues in a report titled *Listening to Latinas: Barriers to High School Graduation* (2009). Here are some of the main points. (Read the full report to gain a greater understanding of the stories associated with the Latina experience.)

Three topics of great consequence to Latinas are:

- Latinas have high aspirations, but too many doubt their ability to reach their goals;

- The Latino community faces many challenges that help to explain the discrepancy between Latinas' dreams and actual expectations; and

- Latinas face particular challenges related to the intersection of their ethnicity and gender.

The report lists recommendations that will bridge this divide:

- Invest in the future of Latino children;

- Connect with role models and engage them in goal-setting;

- Help Latino parents get more involved in the education of their children; and

- Improve efforts to prevent teen pregnancy, including the provision of comprehensive sex education to students.

The National Campaign to Prevent Teen and Unplanned Pregnancy's Latino Initiative's Web site, http://www.thenationalcampaign.org/espanol/ default_eng.aspx, is an invaluable resource. A flagship publication of this organization, *Voices Heard: Adults and Teens Speak Up about Teen Pregnancy* (2007), shares the thoughts of Latino teen parents, both male and female. A common finding by this and many other meticulous reports on Latinos is that parents send conflicting messages to their children or adolescents. For the most part these messages are inherent in their cultural values and heritage. A time-honored custom is that it is acceptable for males to go out on weekends unsupervised, while it is not acceptable for females to go out at all. And if females do go out, they tend to receive a scolding sermon for improper behavior; a male receives a different lecture. For example, the mom might say in a soft voice to the young adult male leaving the house to not commit a bad act—*no anden de traviesos*—or be careful— *tengan mucho cuidado*—or any number of messages that are not seen as reprimands. Better understanding Latino perceptions of and attitudes about certain subjects, such as how differing parental attitudes toward male and female teens leads to pregnancy, gives us a broader perspective from which to operate. The solution in many, if not most cases, is to treat both sexes with the same parental rules and consequences so that they are treated equally and fairly.

Public libraries may contribute to the solutions being offered by 1) becoming aware of these types of serious issues and 2) knowing that they may indeed have a positive impact on the lives of these individuals. Libraries can then be seen as places of enlightenment and connectedness. Some of you may be thinking that this issue is not part of the library domain and should be handled by other organizations that tailor their services to teen pregnancy. Others may feel that it is more than they can handle. There is and probably will always be a precedent for not being remotely aware of this issue or for taking any action. However, I would argue that since this is an issue of serious proportions for Latina teens, we need to address it somehow.

In the library literature, you can find a wealth of headlines about services that don't seem essential to libraries. One example is "Can't Afford a Prom Dress? Try the Local Library." I am not knocking this library's drive in any way but simply pointing out that it's a matter of perspective as to how we define how libraries may create public value among Latina teens.

Gangs and Criminal Behavior

In this section, crime is defined as any type of risky behavior that is illegal and has negative legal and/or social consequences. Lawbreaking activities might include vandalism, stealing, and gang activity—all of which may be intertwined. Malcolm Gladwell shares the following:

> Crime can be more than understood. It can be prevented. There is a broader dimension to this. Judith Harris has convincingly argued that peer influence and community influence are more important than family influence in determining how children turn out. Studies of juvenile delinquency and high school drop-out rates, for example, demonstrate that a child is better off in a good neighborhood and a troubled family than he or she is in a troubled neighborhood and a good family (Gladwell 2000, 167).

In the meantime, Latino parents must understand and acknowledge that Latino students are more likely to attend schools with a large influx of Latinos who reside in neighborhoods with a lower socioeconomic status (SES), low income families, and underfunded schools. As parents they need to familiarize themselves with the elements outside of the household; the same is true for librarians. During my outreach years, I would typically ask participants in community or parent meetings which scenario was best for their adolescent kids. Scenario number one, living with low socioeconomic status but with exceptional parents, or scenario number two, living in a well-to-do community but with dysfunctional parents. The largest part of the audience would raise their hands for scenario number one. After I explained that in fact the opposite was true, a discussion would ensue, focusing on what parents could do to find solutions. Some ideas that came from these dialogues as possible solutions were:

- Get teens involved in academic afterschool programs;
- Matriculate teens into advanced classes;

- Demonstrate to teens that you value education by visiting institutions of higher education on a quarterly basis;

- Join teens while they do their homework; and

- Encourage teens to affiliate with people with positive educational outlooks.

Stories and initiatives pertaining to serving "troubled" Latino teens abound. Too often a negative overtone and expectation plagues them. If society would just spend more time focusing on the positive instead of the negative, wouldn't our efforts be that much more successful? Marcus Buckingham takes the standpoint that you learn more from successful models than negative models (Buckingham 2001). One simple example proves his point. If you are studying marriage, and you want your marriage to be successful, would you study solid, stable couples or carefully look at dysfunctional duos? Obviously, you would learn more from the former. This same principle applies to Latino teens and their associates.

Consider Father Greg Boyle. A simple Google search will retrieve a great deal of information pertaining to this man. A recent article in *Psychology Today* titled "Give Gangs This Day Their Daily Bread" featured Father Greg. He started a bakery business where most of the workers are former gang members and gives them the opportunity to get on their feet and steers them in the right direction of being civic-minded citizens with good moral values and productive members of society. When asked if it is hard to convert gang members, his response was that "our program is only for those who want it. We don't go to them" (Jen 2010, 19).

Teachers, counselors, and police gang units, as well as many other organizations and social service providers, are very familiar with giveaway signs, mannerisms, drawings, and vocabulary used by gang members. For example, consider observing the binders that male Latinos carry for any signs of gang participation. Easy giveaways are the following word and fonts:

SURENOS

𝔖𝔘𝔯𝔢𝔫𝔬𝔰

Sureños loosely translates to "southerner," meaning someone from Southern California who tends to affiliate with gang members.

So what can libraries do about gangs? Consider this story of a former gang member. One of the most vicious Latino gangs known to any California correctional facility is the Mexican Mafia. At one time, a high-ranking member of this criminal organization, nicknamed Boxer, was doing what was expected of its membership. Fortunately Boxer grew tired of this lifestyle and wanted to get out. In his biography, you'll find two sentences to keep in mind when working with troubled Latino teens: "Meanwhile, there was something else that for years had been slowly changing Boxer's outlook on life—books" and "Books were increasing his vocabulary and opening up a whole new world to him." This shows that there is hope and that librarians are facing very different conditions than their predecessors.

For more in-depth accounts of what it entails to be in a gang, consider reading *Father Greg and the Homeboys* by Celeste Fremon (Hyperion 1995), *This Is for the Mara Salvatrucha* by Samuel Logan (Hyperion 2009), and *The Mexican Mafia* by Tony Rafael (Encounter Books 2007).

Dropouts

This is a true story. An elementary school teacher planned a field trip for her third grade class. They were going to visit a nearby museum. Since the school did not budget for these types of field trips, teachers counted on parent volunteers. Only a handful of parents assisted in this endeavor. On the day of the field trip, the teacher lined up the students outside of the classroom and instructed each parent to take the number of students that their vehicle might accommodate. Some parents took two, some three, and some ambitious parents took four. As you can imagine, if a student's parent was part of this entourage, that student, along with his or her best friends, went in that parent's vehicle. The parent then headed with his or her company to the museum. This sorting and picking of friends by students caused a small amount of disorder, as students were crying out loud, "Pick me." After this mess cleared up, two students had not been picked by fellow classmates. They stood there watching as other students happily and cheerfully joined their rides. You should have seen the faces of these two innocent third graders. The teacher, quick to notice this blunder, immediately reacted by saying that they would go with her. How do you suppose the two students felt when they were not selected? What do you think was going through their minds? No one knows, yet they probably thought that they had friends that might point them out. These third graders easily adjusted by joining the teacher and later being reunited with their peers in the museum. The troubling part of this actual scenario is not evident immediately or even during the ensuing moment. It happens years later down the road. This will be a negative memory for these two students. When they are of age to reflect on how they grew up, they recall those moments of happiness, of fear, and of isolation. These types of experiences form a person's attitudes, feelings, and thoughts. And if they have many downbeat encounters, they will likely grow up feeling alienated, being drifters and imprudent. Dropping out is just one possible result of these feelings. Unfortunately, this is the story of what happens to many Latino teens.

What can parents, educators, community members, civic organizations, and libraries do to counter dropout and vagrancy? Obviously, we need to become more relevant by addressing Latino teens' needs. In an article titled "The Crisis Facing Our Boys," Franziska Castillo makes five recommendations:

1. Give boys the same rules as girls;

2. Find him a stand-in big brother;

3. Give him a book;

4. Encourage *orgullo*—pride in his culture; and

5. Invoke a rite of passage to usher your son into manhood.

Young Latino males tend to be very assertive and proud. When forming relationships with Latino teens you need to respect and honor what is of importance to them. One thing that we should know by now is that culture is a better predictor of knowing someone than the language one speaks. When interacting with teens of Mexican heritage, one of the things you might notice is their use of Caló. Caló can be defined as a string of words conceived to represent a unique expression or utterance with a Spanish subtext. In this case the distinction is that what is said is more important than the tone used. The usage of Caló is a long-standing tradition that has passed down from first-generation immigrants to fourth-generation Latinos. Young people often use it as a private language, one only those familiar with Caló will understand. When Latino teens hear you speak in Caló, two things will happen. Depending on your relationship with them, and who you are, they will either come to trust you because you are utilizing one of their modes of being in touch, or they will mock you because they know that you are being phony. So what do you do? Be yourself? (Appendix B contains a small list of common Caló words.)

Many Latino teens drop out, or are pushed out, as some like to characterize it, due to other factors in their lives. One is a lack of role models, especially at a young age. Those role models could be parents, teachers, neighbors, or anyone that made a significant impact on their lives. It could even be a librarian. The potency of role models is that they provide you with a great deal of inspiration and traits that you hope to replicate one day. The role model breeds and instills optimism and hopefulness. Young Latinos who did not have role models in their early years are cheated out of something they should have had, which places them at a disadvantage. Not knowing any better, they may drop out, because in their subconscious, they have no one with positive influences that they would like to emulate. In the absence of positive role models, they easily fall prey to gangs or organized crime, which give them a connection, a sense of belonging, and a sense of power. That's how good kids get involved with bad groups.

Educational Achievement

How can Latino teens have an equal footing in the educational system when there is an unequal playing field? Most Latino teens contend with social, household, educational, and economic challenges that shape how they function in society. When it comes to education, many hurdles make the instructive process taxing on the educational system, society, and heads of household.

How does education interconnect with libraries? If you were in New Hampshire or Alabama, states that have had significant increase in the number of Latinos in recent years, you would probably notice more Latinos in the schools and neighborhoods, due to their physical characteristics or spoken language. Even though these are states with relatively small percentages of Latinos, this growing minority has an impact on society. *Latinos in New England* reveals the long history and great influence that one million plus Latinos have had in these Northern states (Torres 2006).

The following, based on case studies that address education, are some of the major factors that affect the Latino teen's educational experience. In no particular order they are:

- Dropout rate of Latinos as a general group;

- Attending a school with a high concentration of underrepresented students;

- Limited participation in pre-kindergarten programs;

- Less funding for schools with a high percentage of underrepresented groups;

- School curriculum not readily prepared for sudden increase of Latino student body population;

- Latinos representing the largest group of underrepresented students in the student body;

- Latino lower enrollment rates in institutions of higher learning;

- Counselors not recommending vigorous courses;

- Low parent involvement; and

- Implementation of English Language Learners programs.

A scientific study from the Pew Hispanic Center aptly describes the dissimilarity between Latinos of varied backgrounds:

> The bulk of Hispanic youth is of Mexican origin. About 25 percent of Mexican-origin 16 to 19 year-olds have not finished high school and are not enrolled in school. Some of the populations from Central America have higher dropout rates. Nicaraguan-origin youth have lower dropout rates, and many of the populations originating from South America have dropout rates similar to white youth. (Pew Hispanic Center 2004, 1)

If you are in an urban community with a large English Language Learner (ELL) program, know that the odds are against Latino teens graduating from high school. Prominent Latino-based think tanks the Tomás Rivera Policy Institute, Pew Hispanic Center, and National Council for La Raza have all concluded that Latino ELL students are three to four times more susceptible to dropping out than teens who speak English fluently. The troubling warning is that New Americans teens are most likely to not complete school. Based on current indicators, ELL students are more likely to be found in lower grade levels. The middle-tier grade level students are U.S. citizens who might not be enrolled in ELL classes, as they will be bilingual or English dominant.

As for college education, Ricardo Alonso Zaldivar presents the following information: "Latinos don't have enough money, yet many are reluctant to borrow. Family obligations intervene. Parents and teachers provide only lukewarm support" (Zaldivar 2010).

There is and continues to be a serious debate over the best teaching instruction method for first-generation Latino teens who only speak Spanish. Many people claim that bilingual education is your ticket to academic achievement. Others believe that a concentration on English only is your path to success. The empirical data surrounding this issue is seemingly divided. You will arrive at different outcomes depending on who you ask. When patrons ask me what program or courses they should purchase or enroll in to practice their English, my response is "Study a borrowed dictionary for one hour every day." The response may sound unorthodox, but so far, verbal feedback has demonstrated that it works.

On a similar note, in his most recent book Rick Sanchez says that "by being immersed in the language, as painful and difficult as it was, I learned to speak English fluently. When I arrived, there was no English as a Second Language program. Trust me, as my life story shows, kids may need help from a bilingual teacher maybe for a semester or two, but after that they are truly better off with a sink-or-swim 'immersion' curriculum" (2010, 235).

Hate Speech and Hate Crimes

An emerging issue that is slowly gaining momentum is hate and speech crime. Diatribes similar to KKK propaganda actually occur today, with abhorrent offenses being broadcasted through mainstream media and in communities. Some of these actions have led to deaths as the transgression goes from verbal to violent. And with the current debate on illegal immigration taking center stage and becoming heated, we can expect certain acts to become more frequent and widespread. Make sure that your library, as an institution, is in no way associated with these acts. Establish your library as a hate-free and hate-speech-free zone and make sure that message is communicated. Furthermore, ensure that staff do not hold bigoted opinions of Latino teens. Not even the federal government is free of bigoted beliefs. On Friday, August 28, 2009, the Associated Press gave a news account that might be considered a hate crime, if not an irrational idea with a poor choice of words. An article titled "Forest Service warning called racial profiling: Campers told to beware of possible pot growers with 'Tecate beer cans'" was featured on MSNBC.com. A verbatim excerpt:

> Denver – A federal warning to beware of campers in national forests who eat tortillas, drink Tecate beer and play Spanish music because they could be armed marijuana growers.

What is even more alarming is that this press release was issued by the United States Forest Service in Colorado. The Colorado Latino community was up in arms about how a government agency could be so ignorant, shocked by how the press release was written in such a derogatory manner, and how the content singled out Latinos. Without a doubt, staff from the Forest Service need to attend some sensitivity training to avoid blunders of this nature in the future.

Parental Guidance

Another problem that affects the way teens grow up and can have long lasting affects upon them is their parents' level of involvement. Levels of parental involvement and engagement range greatly within the Latino community. Some are very interested and concerned, others may have good intentions but are not familiar with the protocol of things to do, and some have no vested interest in their children's education and believe that it is the school's role to educate and mentor teens. Not much of a difference from the general population perhaps, but coupled with other disadvantages that Latino teens face, lack of parental involvement too often becomes critical. In many cases that is why you find organizations trying to reach out to teens, such as the Boys & Girls Club and the YMCA.

A comment that is often heard from librarians is that "we are not in the parenting business," which leads to the conclusion that programs that mentor teens might not succeed. Why should librarians provide these types of programs? Shouldn't it be someone else who might carry this burden instead of libraries? My response is something that TV host Dr. Phil would say to his patients: "And how is that working for you?" Do you believe that your previous efforts with teens have been a success, and do you believe that you have created public value?

With a great, not just good, curriculum, Latino teens genuinely enjoy leadership events. They learn new skills, appreciate the benefits of being a good citizen, are exposed to opportunities that they did not know existed, and enjoy being around successful people. There are many benefits of getting involved in the issues facing Latino teens beyond the librarian's hope of instilling a love for reading. You may influence a young person to get good grades and attend and graduate from college. You might even be grooming a future librarian.

Chris Anderson, editor in chief of *Wired* magazine, holds that the future of business is selling less of more. In one of the sections of his book *The Long Tail*, "In the Library of Misshelved Books," he explains the faults and tribulations of the organization of library books. Online bookstores have an advantage over physical libraries in that you may find the same items in multiple locations. Anderson goes on to say that "in the world of information science, the tricky question of where to put things is known as the 'ontology problem'" (Anderson 2006, 157). "Ontology" means different things in different disciplines, but for librarians and computer scientists (and for retail store managers, whether they know it or not), it is about ways to organize things. Ironically, the taxonomy of collections, which is at times inflexible, should be constructed and organized according to users' needs. Since public libraries are not meant to be archival institutions, Anderson contends that "in the realm of film and television, 'shelved' means canceled or delayed. Shelves are places where things go to die" (2006, 159). That is why librarians have weeding as part of their duties and responsibilities.

If you do not keep these tips at the forefront, your collection will quickly become irrelevant to the Latino teen community; they will see the same items over and over, with no fresh and new items to browse and hopefully read. A final remark that Anderson makes about libraries is that the lack of organization and failure to be agents of change will be considered "a future proof that libraries make no assumptions about the information landscape of tomorrow" (2006, 160).

Serving Latino teens has a universal benefit in that it may reduce the number of issues that plague Latino communities. But libraries need to reach teens before they are beyond a point of no return. For example, it's common knowledge that an ounce of prevention in the form of sex education yields lower teen pregnancy rates. Partnering with law enforcement will increase your awareness of and prepare you to speak to the dangerous lifestyle of underground and gang activity. What you need to keep in mind is the judgment call. Find out when moderate information is more effective and when a more intense intervention is called for. You can gauge this based on your audience.

Surveyed teens indicate that they have a good relationship with their parents, but because of cultural values and the fear of being caught with one, they don't use contraceptives. Since it's the teen who is at the center of this matter, libraries and other organizations should interact directly with teens in a sensible manner. In the case of gang activity, your audience should be the parents. The teens have heard the warnings before; you won't make any headway with them. Hopefully the message will be instilled in the back of their minds, but we need to be proactive and constantly remind them what a "good Samaritan" is. In most cases, you are more likely to have a greater impact with the parents. Unless there are no obvious open signs of gangs, parents aren't going to pick up on the symbols or paraphernalia. That is where the partnership with law enforcement or library experts comes in. They can distinguish realities from myths and must, most importantly, challenge parents on what they can do to identify, educate, and combat this social ill. I am not preaching that we engage vigorously in these subjects, but since they happen to be focal issues of the Latino community, we cannot ignore their significance.

After reading this chapter you may assume your role as a librarian leans more toward that of a social services provider than a traditional library service provider. "They didn't teach this in library school" is a common aphorism among librarians when a new service model or best practice approach is included in our job description. I hope that you recall the quote found at the beginning of this chapter as a guiding principle. The fact is, our roles are changing and will continue to change. If we do not keep abreast of social issues, libraries will lose ground as places to congregate, study, learn, network, and develop lifelong learning skills.

The following chapter leads us to the focal purpose of relationship building with both teens and parents so that libraries are very much aligned with their needs and wants.

References

Anderson, Chris. 2006. *The long tail: Why the future of business is selling less of more*. New York: Hyperion.

Blatchford, Chris. *The black hand*. 2008. New York: HarperCollins.

Buckingham, Marcus. 2001. *Now, discover your strengths*. New York: Free Press.

Castillo, Franziska. 2006. The crisis facing our boys. *Latina Magazine*, November, 92.

Forest Service warning called racial profiling: Campers told to beware of possible pot growers with "Tecate beer cans." 2009. The Associated Press, August 28. http://www.msnbc.msn.com/id/32600601/ns/us_news -life/t/forest-service-warning-called-racial-profiling/ [accessed March 16, 2012].

Garcia, June, and Susan Kent. 2009. The challenge of change: Report to the mayor's task force on the revitalization and future of the Chattanooga-Hamilton County Bicentennial Library. www .chattanooga.gov [accessed March 16, 2012].

Gladwell, Malcolm. 2000. *The tipping point.* New York: Little, Brown.

Kim, Jen. 2010. Give gangs this day their daily bread. *Psychology Today*, January/February, 19.

National Hispanic Medical Association. 2009. *Report on health disparities and Hispanics leadership summit series*. Washington, D.C.: National Hispanic Medical Association. http://www.nhmamd .org/component/content/article/16-speech/118-a-report-on-health- disparities-and-hispanics-leadership-summit-series [accessed March 16, 2012].

National Women's Law Center. 2009. *Listening to Latinas: Barriers to high school graduation*. Washington, D.C.: National Women's Law Center.

Pew Hispanic Center. 2004. *Latino teens staying in high school: A challenge for all generations*. Washington, D.C.: Pew Hispanic Center.

Sanchez, Rick. 2010. *Conventional idiocy: Why the new America is sick of old politics*. New York: Penguin.

Torres, Andrés. 2006. *Latinos in New England*. Philadelphia: Temple University Press.

Vexler, E. 2007. *Voices heard: Latino adults and teens speak up about teen pregnancy*. Washington, DC: National Campaign to Prevent Teen Pregnancy.

Zaldivar, Ricardo Alonso. 2010. *AP – Univision poll: College dreams for Hispanics.* http://www.msnbc.msn.com/id/32600601/ns/us_news-life/ t/forest-service-warning-called-racial-profiling/ [accessed March 16, 2012].

3

Relationship Building

Do not wait for leaders; do it alone, person to person.

—Mother Teresa, in *Living a Five Star Life*

Joey Rodger, former president of the Urban Libraries Council once stated that "libraries are in the library business. They are also in the community business." If libraries do not have constant and sustained contacts and a web of networks with teens and teen-related groups, the profession will not be socially, educationally, and politically astute. There is more to the library business than library business. Peter Schwartz confesses in *The Art of the Long View* that "normal business is about products, services, and the exchange of cash. But in an economy where knowledge and information directly improve the bottom line, personal relationships become much more important" (Schwartz 1996, 78). Libraries are in the relationship business because there is a reciprocal understanding that both patrons and libraries want and wish for a win-win association. Patrons embrace the library and utilize its many services and programs, and libraries flourish.

Sometimes it seems as if librarians have missed the point in serving Latino teens. Could it be that for far too long libraries have affirmed that rendering library services to Spanish speakers, which lumped adults, teens, and children together, simply meant that they had Spanish collections, hired Spanish-speaking staff, and offered bilingual programs? Nowadays, that approach could not be farther from the mark. Yet, many librarians continue to consider this population to be one homogenous group.

Parent Involvement

Building relationships with Latino teens also means building relationships with parents, guardians, and households. There are many schools of thought as to why parents need to be involved with and included in the welfare of Latino teens. It really boils down to the fact that if the parent, guardian, or household approves of what the teen is trying to do, then it is ok to do whatever the situation calls for. Parents will have a sense of being stakeholders in their teen's upbringing and at times enforce their beliefs on something that they may disagree with.

For example, if a male Latino teen wants to join the football team, he might have to run it by both parents for approval. Chances are that they will both agree, because it will keep the teen engrossed in a positive extracurricular sport. The conflicting side of this approval process is when the teen wants to do something that the parents do not approve of, yet the male Latino teen insists on doing it anyway. One such example is hanging out with friends who might not be a positive influence and are known as troublemakers. This dialogue will be heated, as both sides will not be on the same page in terms of why the male Latino teen may or may not hang out with these acquaintances. The two types of situations go hand in hand. With mutual decision making, sometimes there will be agreement, and sometimes there will be disagreement.

Serving teens should be and can be much simpler than serving the general Latino population. Since there aren't as many impediments such as language and cultural barriers as there could be with past generations, you will be able to interact with Latino teens with your standard style of communication. As shown in the previous chapter, Latino teens are and will continue to gain proficiency in English. At some point, you will reach a crossroad when you must decide how you are going to go about serving Latino teens.

According to a book traditionally found in most public libraries, *Etiquette* by Peggy Post, "although many people believe that the old adage 'when in Rome, do as the Romans do' means that international visitors and residents in our country should immediately adopt to American customs, it is thoughtful if we try to learn about some of our visitors' cultures, too. It is only courteous to respect the practices of others by participating in them as you are able to do so" (Post 1997). As you know, libraries exist to render relevant and responsive library services and programs. That is why it is imperative that libraries take to heart the notion of building relationships with people of Latino heritage—especially if they want to earn their patronage, respect, and trust.

Latino Teens Are No Surprise

As mentioned previously, we cannot say that this Latino teen population wave is an unprecedented or sudden demographic transformation. In hindsight we should have been slowly preparing for how to work closely with this growing population of Latino teens. If the traditional Latino teen generational trend continues, the next area of study should be to figure out exactly what services and collections a third- or fourth-generation Latino teen is going to need and want. Or more specifically, how is the library profession going to make progress in our educational system to ensure that all young children and young adults, whatever their background, develop a lifelong love of books, reading, and learning? In addition, how are educational service providers going to guarantee that their imaginations are stimulated by the challenge of offering pleasurable reading, viewing, and listening experiences. Will they need to be identified as Latino services? My hunch is that by this time, Latino youth will be mainstream, or even the majority. They will take pride in their culture but will be interested in what mainstream culture has to offer and shy away from being typecast to cultural services.

Another cultural characteristic of first-generation Latino teens is that they might not pressure or pursue additional information from library staff due to their passivity, lack of assertiveness, or not wishing to partake in confrontational behavior. This goes back to the concept instilled in them by their parents of not disrespecting figures of authority. The reverse is evident in second- (or greater) generation Latino teens, because they know that they are empowered and within their rights and liberties to follow up if they do not find the information they are seeking. This simple distinction should be noted by library staff and used to determine whether to possibly trail or join a patron in quest for desired resources.

If you take serving Latino teens to heart, you might notice that many of the reports and studies cited do not derive from the library profession. We need to expand our horizon and reading material to truly dissect the issues affecting this segment of the population. If we don't proceed with such actions, it might qualify as what Albert Einstein would coin as insanity—which he decodes as doing the same thing over and over again and expecting different results. A manifestation of this attitude is seen quite frequently in librarianship when staff feels that "what is ours is ours. What is yours is subject to change."

Because you are reading this book, you may have outgrown some aspects of your job. If so, you are in a premier position to build relationships. To cite a simple example from libraryland, we have outgrown the card catalog and now use online public access catalogs (OPACs). Somehow you and your colleagues made your jobs more efficient by venturing into this new service point. We have also introduced multiple types of literature genres that at one point were considered eerie or out-of-bounds for libraries, such as genre fiction or graphic novels. Then came along CDs, VHS tapes, and now DVDs. The future may and will offer new electronic portable devices. We have endured and embraced many changes—successfully.

New Competencies Required

According to Richard M. Lerner, PhD, there are six strengths that will nurture and enhance positive development in teens for a prosperous future with healthy habits. They are:

- *Competence*: the ability to act effectively in school, in social situations, and at work;
- *Confidence*: an internal sense of overall self-worth and efficacy;
- *Connection*: positive bonds with people and social institutions;
- *Character*: respect for society and cultural rules, an inner moral compass;
- *Caring*: a sense of sympathy and empathy for others and a commitment to social justice; and
- *Contribution*: the capacity of teenagers to participate effectively by caring for themselves, so as not to be a drain on others, and by giving of themselves at home, in the community, and in civic life (Lerner 2007, 35).

Are we promoting these developmental strengths? Even though these concepts were meant for the general teen population, they are easily transferable and applicable to Latino teens. Are we incorporating them into our knowledge base and employing them to better serve teens?

Often Latino teens want more than good literature, services, programs, and space—they desire the feeling of belonging. If library systems focus on them, even slightly cater to them, services tend to expand naturally over time and make a tremendous difference.

Of course, make sure that you don't bite off more than you can chew. For example, let's say you want to be a marathon runner. Well, do you have a trainer? Do you already run? Do you work out? If you are not already doing any of the above, you are setting yourself up for failure. A great deal of the professional literature pronounces that you begin building relationships when you commence talking with the customers, community, community leaders, and so forth. I find this approach insufficient. You might be able to reach a mutual understanding that way, but if there is no prior commitment to serving Latino teens, there will be no progress in serving Latino teens. Unless there is a *partnership*, a form of project sustainability on both sides, and value added to any of the participating organizations, you would be just as well off without making the outreach effort. Like the hopeful marathon runner, libraries should not skip steps in reaching out to Latino teens. Doing so will result in a halfhearted process and results.

As the opening quote puts it, do things on a personal level. Latinos generally like the human touch. This means offering a Chicano handshake, hugging, and even kissing at times. While this might seem awkward to non-Latinos, it is perfectly natural for most Latinos. According to Tracy Novinger, "personal relationships are very important, and telephone interviews are neither common nor very welcome" (2001, 134). However, if you read some of the recommendations offered by Latino organizations or telemarketers, you will see that their first approach is to conduct surveys over the telephone or in the actual library. This approach is flawed. Telephone interviews may be seen as suspicious by first-generation Latinos. Second-generation Latinos might avoid the telephone interview altogether. Conducting surveys in the library is equivalent to preaching to the choir. That is why extending your services should be conducted off library grounds.

Fostering Awareness

You cannot change what you are not aware of. Your first step in building relationships is to build your awareness. Library staff has a dual reading obligation that needs to be converted to knowledge that will fuel understanding. We may read about Latino teens in books like this one. We may also read *with* them, including literature they enjoy reading or asking them what their preferences are.

The following questions will help you evaluate your services and programs to Latino teens. The questions present thresholds that should be considered when rendering library services to Latino teens and are not necessarily consistent with standard practices. Therefore, it is recommended that library staff use them as discussion points and measures to audit and gauge services to Latino teens:

1. Do you know the cultural, social, economic, psychological, technological, and sexual characteristics of Latino teens?

2. Do your peers know the social, economic, psychological, techno-logical, and sexual characteristics of Latino teens?

3. How will the library industry survive when teens may obtain what-ever information they are seeking from multiple sources without consulting the library?

4. How do you create public value in the Latino teen community?

5. Is serving Latino teens a paradigm shift for you institution?

6. How can the profession increase the number of Latino librarians to better serve the communities we currently serve and will serve in the future?

7. Is learning something new such as how to serve Latino teens tak-ing a toll on you and your organization?

8. Since society is changing faster than the library profession, how can we assure ourselves that we are kept abreast of, embrace, and offer the latest trends to our patrons while eliminating tradition-al services that no longer are deemed imperative or essential to our profession, yet are still being conducted by many of our col-leagues?

9. What lies ahead with Latino teens at your library? Does this idea alarm you?

10. Do you feel as if every time you get things figured out, someone changes them again?

11. What duty of your current job could you stop doing in order to start better serving Latino teens?

One of the recent research publications to address the needs of Latino teens is the *2009 What Works for Latino Students*. An abstract of the com-pendium report asserts that "given the importance of college degree comple-tion for U.S. society and economic competitiveness, meeting the country's future human capital and workforce needs make it imperative to improve outcomes for Latino students. As public attention is focused on achievement gaps in education, educators and policymakers search for what they can do to improve education outcomes for Latino students" (Santiago 2009, 2).

Relationship building can be called a self-concordant effort; in other words, the goal is pursued out of a deep personal conviction or interest. If you don't feel that you should be building relationships as part of your daily job, then you are not suited for librarianship. According to *Latinos and*

Public Library Perceptions, "Latinos are more concerned with friendly staff service than Spanish language access" (Flores and Pachon 2008, 13).

Proactive Is the Key to Success

Advocating for free reading versus prescribed reading has its pros and cons with Latino teens. It might sound comical, but as parents we have all gone through this episode in life. Answer one of your child's requests with a "no," and they will try to find a "yes" for doing it. Tell someone "don't run in the library," and it will encourage them to actually run or to run after you turn the other way. Reverse psychology may play more to your advantage, and you can probably arrive at the same results without undermining, stereotyping, or restricting Latino teens.

When building relationships with Latino teens, we need to put a positive spin on many of our practices. One prime example of when you can practice this strategy is when creating guidelines for your teen section. Instead of posting things such as "No Food," "No Drinks," "No Loud Talking," or "No This or No that," consider phrasing guidelines positively, as in the example that follows.

The Enterprise Library of the Las Vegas Clark County Library District (NV), which I happen to manage, with the assistance of a stellar Children Services assistant and input from the actual teen community, drew up a few parameters that are positive in scope. Four of the principles that are prominently displayed in the teen section are: *Respect the space, other guests, and library staff; Use school language and your library voice; One person per chair;* and *Get involved.* In the few years that we have had the teen zone, we have had only a few minor incidents. To be honest, the bulk of the headaches come from adults wanting to use that space.

Not addressing Latino teens with a cultural connotation may take you farther than force-feeding them diversity and/or ethnic programs and services. If you have a Latino teen constituency within your service area, chances are they will take advantage of your services to their fullest potential.

In the September 2009 issue of *Vanidades*, the number one women's beauty, fashion, and lifestyle magazine in the U.S. Hispanic-speaking market, you will find an article titled "¡Revelados! Los Secretos de la Personas Felices." A basic translation of this headline is "Revealed, the Secrets of Happy People." The article outlines 10 steps that contribute to the happiness that Latinos exhibit. Loosely translated they are:

1. Forget the past;
2. Live in the present;

3. Cultivate your relationships;

4. Accept yourself;

5. Use your talents;

6. Count your blessings;

7. Control your mind;

8. Enjoy the small things;

9. Don't judge—understand; and

10. Make others happy.

During the stretch of the day, I have the luxury of working in various departments, either to fill in when someone is conducting a program, staff the circulation or customer services desk if library is short staffed, or simply to wander about to keep an eye on things. During one of my shifts I was working in the children's department assisting families and children with their educational or recreational needs. Ironically, a Latino family approached the desk and asked me if I spoke Spanish. I responded "yes," and answered all of their questions. They were mainly interested in obtaining new library cards for their two children. I explained the process, which involves completing the library card application online. Keep in mind that we had been speaking in Spanish all along. When I took them to the computer station, I instructed the caregiver to select Español and then ¡Inscribase ahora para obtener una tarjeta gratuita de la biblioteca! Somewhat to my surprise, the mother rebutted me by saying that she preferred to complete the online library card application in English. She continued her sentence in Spanish by saying, "How do you expect me to learn English if I do not practice it?" Needless to say, I took her to the English version. This indicates how many Latino households are able and willing to practice English, while retaining Spanish.

Humor

In a September 2009 episode of *The View* George Lopez found the Latino in everyone, even President Barack Obama. Lopez claimed that President Obama shares many Latino characteristics. For example, he lives in a house that is not his—very Latino; spends money that he doesn't have; is bailing people out—that's very Mexican; and his mother-in-law is helping raise the kids. This is the type of humor that works for everyone, especially Latino teens, as it is not insulting nor does it undermine the presidency.

While much of George Lopez's comedy can be categorized as stereotypical, his generalizations about the lifestyles of many Latinos are not far from the truth.

Action Learning Activities

One service that has the backing of students from lower socioeconomic backgrounds is Upward Bound. Review their services and types of products and you will notice some similarities. Networking, partnering, or working in collaboration may prove to be beneficial strategies for your respective library. As an Upward Bound alumnus I can vouch for this program. Had it not been for its presence during my high school years, there is no telling where I would currently be. What Upward Bound provided to me was homework assistance, mentors, tutoring, and an educational summer camp at an institution of higher education to introduce and encourage college attendance. This program did pay off in my case.

The concept of action learning is that you learn by doing, not necessarily listening and seeing. Upward Bound provides students with an avenue in which they will receive tutoring at their local school, attend conferences, and take educational tours. They are exposed to successful individuals from their schools, mainly teachers and counselors. The program strives to instill the importance of attending college and encourages a culture of academia so teens are determined, willing, and prepared to take on the experience of attending institutions of higher education.

When meeting with Latino teens head-on, keep in mind their cultural, social, economical, psychological, technological, and sexual needs. Do not automatically assume they have diversity issues, and don't send every Latino request to the diversity officer or committee. Tackle them right there and then, as their needs for the most part are not diversity related. If this new service point doesn't fall within your comfort zone, practice the longest-standing library tradition and belief: we are there to serve all. One of the highest-ranking Latinas to retire from the military, Consuelo Kickbusch Castillo, declares that "rather than striving to fit someone else's preconceived ideas of whom and what we should be or how we should look, we can choose to appreciate ourselves now. We can celebrate our own uniqueness, our own special weight, height and hair color, our own ethnic heritage" (2003, 22).

Building relationships is taxing, demanding, and rewarding. As a librarian you have the opportunity to build relationships that range from interacting with parents to exchanging ideas with others from a variety of associations or organizations. Due to the ever changing and unprecedented economic climate that we find ourselves in, it is important, now more than ever, to give people a handshake and not our traditional handout. Many other associations or organizations are facing the same dilemma, and if we can all agree and rely on each other, the easier the task of serving Latino teens.

The following chapter will introduce you to exciting best practices that will pick up the pace of your understanding and awareness of and improve your presence with Latino teens. Our discussion leads us to vital services affecting Latino teens today.

References

Castillo, Consuelo Kickbusch. 2003. *Journey to the future: A roadmap for success for youth*. Raleigh, NC: Liberty Publishing Group.

Flores, Edward, and Harry Pachon. 2008. *Latinos and public library perceptions*. California: Tomás Rivera Policy Institute.

Hernandez, G.B. 2009. ¡Revelados! Los Secretos de la Personas Felices. *Vanidades*, September, 101.

Lerner, Richard M. 2007. *The good teen*. New York: Stonesong Press.

Mahalik, Betty. 2008. *Living a five star life: The secret to finding greater joy and reaching your full potential*. Naperville, IL: Simple Truths.

Novinger, Tracy. 2001. *Intercultural communication: A practical guide*. Austin: University of Texas Press.

Post, Peggy. 1997. *Etiquette*. 16th Edition. New York: HarperCollins.

Santiago, Deborah. 2009. *2009 What works for Latino students*. Washington, D.C.: ¡Excelencia in Education!.

Schwartz, Peter. 1996. *The art of the long view: Planning for the future in an uncertain world*. New York: Doubleday.

4

Services

*It is clear that youth should have alternative
outlets for recreation and association
and that these alternatives should be readily available.*

—Ray Oldenburg, *The Great Good Place*

The new rules for serving Latino teens may or may not surprise you. Evidence and empirical findings leading up to 2010 indicate that now is a good time to reconcile all of the confusing opinions that exist about serving Latinos, especially Latino teens. The conventional wisdom about serving Latinos in general is neither applicable nor transferable when serving Latino teens.

Conventional wisdom suggested that to serve Latinos, you offer Spanish-language collections, bilingual personnel, and bilingual services and programs. It even went so far as to state that you needed to put the Spanish-language collection front and center so that customers would have accessible collections. If your current practice is based on conventional wisdom, it will likely be a detriment to your teen services, because conventional wisdom mainly addresses Spanish-speaking first-generation adults of Latino heritage. Actually, the conventional approach does not even fully apply to today's Spanish-speaking first-generation adults of Latino heritage. This chapter dispels the concepts behind the conventional wisdom in their entirety.

Have a Service Plan

A common response or reaction I hear to suggestions for serving Latino teens is "we have tried that in the past with no success." I will venture to say that the previous endeavors were planned without input from Latino teens, which resulted in no real stakeholders to advance that particular service or program. Previous attempts in serving Latino teens are no indication of future initiatives, because both society and the profession have drastically changed.

José Aponte, executive director of the San Diego Library District, spoke during the 2009 Nevada Library Association Annual Conference. His talk, "Dancing with the Elephants: Stay Relevant in Extraordinary Times," suggested that every community has its plan. Find yours and tailor it to your community. Look for planning documents. Aponte lists the top six issues of most municipalities:

1. Public Safety;
2. Health Care;
3. Education;
4. Jobs;
5. Housing; and
6. Traffic.

There are three areas that you should acquaint yourself with to ensure the success of services to Latino teens. The three areas are the state or level of culture, your Strategic Plan, and technology.

When the economy was robust, libraries flourished. Now that some of those same libraries are in budget slashing mode, services and programs are sadly being reduced and/or abolished. Coupled with the fact that the Internet seems to have taken the place of adult, teen, and children services and collections, traditional library services have lost much ground in recent years with one notable exception—services to teens. This segment of the population has grown more than any age group, and services to teens have also grown. With this trend in mind, libraries need a sustainable and functional approach to serving Latino teens.

With the rising number of Latino teens come increasing needs for a support system. The Aspen Institute study titled *Informing Communities: Sustaining Democracy in the Digital Age* states that "a common theme is that readers learn about poor people, labor unions, ethnic minorities, and youth only through stories framed by conflict" (Knight Commission 2009, 54). Latino teens are most definitely caught up in this scenario.

As librarians working with what might be considered new constituents within our demographic service areas, we need to place more emphasis on hard data rather than the speculation that we oftentimes resort to. Case studies allow us to make educated decisions for future library trends and services based on input from those involved in the process. Shifting service priorities to teens not only fosters a greater awareness of the library profession among youth, but leads to and benefits our existing economic base and positions us for long-term literacy gains. Latino teens are ready when you are.

Strategic Planning

The information and statistics presented so far provide a snapshot of the Latino teen population and can help you better design and implement a Strategic Plan. The best way to secure your place in the Latino teen market is through well-executed planning. Be strategic and ensure that staff members are fit for their duties and responsibilities to carry out services to Latino teens.

Do you want your library system to improve in a certain area—let's say increase the number of teens attending a program or increase the circulation of your graphic novels? Then put yourself on a quota system to improve services to teens. You will see momentum build as positive results become evident. Of course, during the course of the Strategic Planning process, be realistic by setting attainable goals.

Now that everything seems to be an urgent matter, you need to prioritize your duties and responsibilities. The answer: a Strategic Plan. This type of goal setting can boost support by addressing your community needs. It's a simple process that helps librarians tackle the community needs and a gentle approach that helps you stop taking on too many irrelevant tasks.

When planning services, incorporate the following processes:

1. Needs assessment;
2. Strategy/stratification;
3. Components identification;
4. Implementation/prescription.

The Latino population has increased significantly throughout most of the country. The one region that has seen the greatest soar is the South. Libraries in the South need to pay particular attention to their local demographic shifts so that their services are properly aligned with their constituents. For example, the Southern Education Foundation found that "from 2007 to 2008, for instance, 44 percent of the approximately 600,000 new Latino residents in the Southern states came from other regions of the country" (Southern Education Foundation 2010, 13). Although the report did not specify exact grade levels, we can assume that some of these students fall within the teen category. These new demographics suggest a need for new services. If growth of Latino students continues, librarians should consider this a portent of things to come as all signs are indicating that underrepresented groups will become the majority.

The bottom line is that things that get measured get done. That is why it is important to start and/or follow a Strategic Plan with clearly stated, concrete goals. This approach ensures that the teen services are included and actually receive the proper attention, resources, and spaces. A Strategic Plan should be both tactical and practical. As with other new library initiatives, it may take a few weeks or months before you see tangible results from your efforts to serve Latino teens. Give it a few months to see whether there's a positive effect.

Pythagoras, a famous Greek philosopher, stated that "the oldest, shortest words—'yes' and 'no'—are those which require the most thought." Strategic Plans prescribe which services should be said yes and no to. Libraries today find themselves in unprecedented tight situations due to the downturn of the economy and need to make decisions with caution and adversity. Strategic Plans help keep you on track by moving everyone in the same direction. The following examples of Strategic Plans show how teen services can and have been incorporated. The bottom line is, if your services are convenient, welcoming, and tailored to teens, they will come—Latino or not.

Chattanooga Public Library

One example of successful Strategic Planning was done at Chattanooga-Hamilton County Bicentennial Library. In a nutshell, the mayor of Chattanooga-Hamilton County sought consultants to find a way to revitalize the library system. The process involved interviewing more than eight hundred Chattanooga residents. After the consultants completed an exhaustive fact-finding mission, they recommended goals and objectives that would assist the library system in Chattanooga to become a vibrant and thriving service. Some of the suggested goals and objectives involved and included teen issues. Teens were an integral segment of Chattanooga, and they were going to be targeted. (Read more about this program on the city's Web site: http://www.chattanooga.gov/default.asp [accessed March 18, 2012].)

Las Vegas-Clark County Library District

The Las Vegas-Clark County Library District (NV) has had Strategic Plans for quite some time. One of their most recent Strategic Plans incorporated measureable goals and objectives. In addition to including these goals and objectives, it holds staff and management accountable for reaching these benchmarks. Below you will find what they elected to focus on regarding teens and measurements for being successful.

Goal 7   Young Adults will have materials and programs that respond to their current interests and provide pleasurable reading, viewing, and listening experiences. (Stimulate the Imagination: Reading, Viewing, and Listening for Pleasure)

7.1:   By FY10/11, the circulation of young adult materials will increase from 409,927 (FY06/07) to 451,000.

7.2:   Annually, a minimum of 5,000 young adults (ages 12–17) will attend a library sponsored or co-sponsored program in library or virtually.

7.3:   Annually, at least 250 young adult programs will be presented by youth services staff (Dubberly Garcia Associates 2008).

Technology

There are many areas that could be discussed in regards to Latino teens, but here we focus on technology. Why technology? Why not literacy? Why not ESL? We have already seen that Latino teens are tech-savvy. Latino teens from upscale communities as well as those who reside in underprivileged parts of town are connected, mainly through mobile technology. With one device they are able to download music, ringtones, games, applications, wallpaper, or whatever else is available through their providers. Perhaps more importantly, with mobile phones, education resources are readily available that allow teens to accomplish more by working or staying connected together.

You may have noticed that many articles and much professional discourse are preoccupied with the end of the book and libraries. To some degree, they are right—particularly if libraries do not drastically tailor library services to their tech-savvy teens. Writer Daniel Akst says that "lending libraries will have to figure out a new mission; the time is not far off when the typical 10-year-old will have the equivalent of the Library of Alexandria in her backpack" (2010, A28).

There is a common misconception that teens on social networking sites are up to no good. On the contrary, they are generally hanging out with friends rather than meeting strangers or predators. It is important to comprehend the impact of technology on Generation Z. While Generation X learned about computers while completing high school and Generation Y picked it up somewhat earlier, Generation Z is fully fluent in everything electronic. For example, according to one of the most recent publications by the Knight Commission, "English-speaking Latinos currently represent especially active population of mobile Web users. Between the end of 2007 and early 2009, 47 percent of English-speaking Latinos access the Internet via a mobile device as opposed to 32 percent of the general population" (Knight Commission 2009, 5).

While books will continue to exist in the foreseeable future, Latino teens will welcome new technology. At one point some journalists were up in arms because public libraries were weeding classics such as Shakespeare. Now those journalists are discovering the realities of reading as their own format is quietly disappearing. If a giant retailer like Amazon is advancing Kindles and electronic books, it will only be a matter of time before most teens carry such devices. In light of this trend, these same people may not use the library, if the library isn't technologically equipped. Borders bookstores were forced to close due to many reasons, but one main factor was their lack of electronic devices.

As a librarian, you have a brand to advertise, which is the name of your institution—the Anytown Public Library. Librarians are also tasked with promoting their product, which is their resources and services—books, music, DVDs, story time, databases, and so forth. What if you were to leaf through a book that covered the subject of things that were popular at a given point in time and then became outdated? This book does exist, and it has many models applicable to our profession: *Obsolete: An Encyclopedia of Once-Common Things Passing Us By*. The list of library-related products in this work includes books, dictionaries, encyclopedias, microfilm, newspapers, slide projectors, thesauruses, typewriters, and videos. Aren't some of these traditional library services and products no longer offered? The one that hit me was books. The author includes books on the list because "according to a 2007 poll conducted by the Associated Press, more than a quarter of Americans read less than one book per year; if they're reading at all" (Grossman 2009).

Short-form reading is gaining ground on long-term reading. That is one reason why social networking sites and the Internet are becoming more accepted and customary with today's teens. Jeff Bezos, founder of Amazon. com, has his own take on books and technology:

Newsweek: "Do you think that the ink-on-paper book will eventually go away?"

Bezos: "I do. I don't know how long it will take."

Newsweek: "Do you still read books on paper?"

Bezos: "Not if I can help it."

Texting and e-mailing have become commonplace among Latino teens due to their need to communicate and socialize. Meanwhile, their parents, while slow to adapt to this digital technology, see the necessity and efficiency of technology and therefore embrace the fact that their children reap the benefits of technology and are connected to both family members and friends alike. *The U.S. Hispanic Market* illustrates where 12- to 17-year-olds are accessing the Internet. Home, library, and school were the three locations that they studied. Interestingly enough, the "library" location scored the lowest percentage among both genders. Hispanic boys used the library 10.3 percent of the time, while Hispanic girls used it 9.4 percent of the time. Home was the first choice, and school followed at second. As we ponder how libraries may become relevant to Latino teens, remember that they do have access, but it may not necessarily be in your physical building.

The usage of social networking sites by Latino teens is more straightforward. MySpace and Facebook are frequented the most by Hispanics who prefer English to Spanish or have no preference. Advertising Age's 2009 Hispanic Fact Pack concurs with the usage of both. What was most surprising is that Twitter is on the lower tier of sites used by Latino teens. In this study, all social networking sites were rated equally among the three types of categories that are distinguished by preference language. This is clear evidence that teens are using social networking sites, but no distinction was made if it were through a computer or mobile technology.

For the sake of comparison, let's review similar information from Mexico, the country of origin of the highest number of Latinos residing in this country. In May 2010, AMIPCI (loosely translated, Mexican Internet Association) published their annual study, which provides a picture of Internet usage from various parts of the country, including an abbreviated profile and principal habits. Statistics from this study are included to show Internet usage in Mexico and how it might positively or negatively affect Mexican Americans' Internet usage in the United States.

Some of the major findings as they pertain to teens are:

- 12–19-year-olds represent the age group that uses the Internet the most at 68 percent. In 2008 the percentage was 63 percent;

- 7 out of every 10, or 68 percent of people between 12 and 19 used the Internet. This represents 21 percent of Mexico's population; and

- 28 percent of Internet users accessed it from an Internet cafe or from public access. In 2008, 34 percent of Internet users accessed it from an Internet cafe or from public access. The report did not speculate on the reason for the decrease in such usage in 2009.

Some of the secondary findings as they relate to the general population of Mexico are:

- 63 percent of households do not own a computer;

- 37 percent of households do own a computer;

- 55 percent of males use the Internet;

- 45 percent of females use the Internet;

- 20–24-year-olds represent the age group that use the Internet the second most at 61 percent. In 2008 the percentage was 55 percent;

- 75 percent of Internet users use the it mainly to send and receive e-mails;

- 51 percent of Internet users download music as their main activity when online; and

- 56 percent of Internet users access it from home. In 2008, 48 percent of Internet users accessed it from home.

The Internet offers Mexicans a wide assortment of resources, beyond books and literature, not readily available at the local library. Many of the sites they visit are seductive in that they find "stuff" that is relevant to them in the pleasure or leisure of a communal place. Instead of competing with the Internet and focusing too much on your electronic resources, libraries should enter the social networking scene as that is where their patrons are. If your library has a Web site, have you ever wondered how you may increase those hits? Make a presence of some sort on the most visited social networking sites, such as Facebook, and watch as the number of hits skyrockets with the same information simply by utilizing sites that exist beyond the library. The catch—you need to staff this service point. In appendix C you will find a short list of sites that may be useful for your library's Web site.

Teen Tech Week is a national initiative aimed at teens, librarians, educators, parents, and other concerned adults to encourage teens to take advantage of libraries' nonprint resources. The library profession recognizes that teens' use of nonprint resources is increasing on a daily basis. This suggests that libraries can still be relevant in the future, the difference being that most of the resources will be electronic instead of in print. This is reality for teens, yet some tenured librarians are still trying to hold on to the traditional print materials.

Think Outside the Wall

One of the most recent studies commissioned by the Institute of Museum and Library Services that characterized the Internet use patterns of individuals, families, and communities is *Opportunity for All: How the American Public Benefits from Internet Access at U.S. Libraries*. Although it did not specifically address teen library usage, it did make some observations on Latino library use. The following relevant findings show that the Latino community should not be taken for granted. According to the report, people of Latino or Hispanic origin:

- Had a higher rate of using the Internet while traveling by a factor of 1.67 compared to non-Latinos;

- Had higher odds of taking computer classes by a factor of 2.31 compared to non-Latinos;

- Had higher odds of applying to college or certified programs by a factor of 1.76 compared to non-Latinos;

- Were more likely to apply for financial aid by a factor of 1.76 compared to non-Latinos;

- Had higher rates of engaging in online learning activities by a factor of 1.79 compared to non-Latinos;

- Were more likely to use the library for creating resumes by a factor of 1.80 compared to non-Latinos;

- Had higher odds of seeking diet information by a factor of 1.57 compared to non-Latinos;

- Had higher odds of paying bills online by a factor of 1.84 compared to non-Latinos; and

- Had higher odds of maintaining personal Web sites or blogs by a factor of 1.68 compared to non-Latinos.

Remember, technology is a double-edged sword. Jim Collins (2001) noted that 80 percent of great companies did not mention technology among the top five concepts that made them great—but did agree that technology assisted them in becoming great. However, William Powers has seemingly uncovered why technology is generally so addictive. Here is his line of reasoning:

- "The more connected we are, the more we depend on the world outside ourselves to tell us how to think and live."

- "The goal is no longer to be 'in touch' but to erase the possibility of ever being out of touch."

- "The more connected a society gets, the easier it is to become a creature of that connectedness."

- "Though much of what keeps us hoping is unavoidable—the demands of work and other inflexible obligations— a fair amount is pure, self-created bustle. Why check the inbox ten times an hour on a Saturday, when once will do?" (Powers 2010)

The degree to which you are willing to serve Latino teens with technology is important. Not only does it suggest to Latino teens that you value them, it also indicates the amount of resources you will need to reallocate. I use the term "reallocate" because most library systems throughout the country are experiencing financial difficulties and are not raising new funds; the second-best alternative is to shift resources from within. If you are finding that teens are not frequenting your library or you are not satisfied with the number of teens in your library, you need to reach out to organizations and associations that have a captive audience. That way, you and that group can plan programs or services that will mutually benefit both. Even if the activity that both of you agreed upon does not take place at the library, you are actively introducing and encouraging the use of libraries.

It is regrettable that there is so little information or research on such a large constituency as Latinos in the library. The library community has not produced any significant amount of literature that addresses the issues of Latinos, much less Latino teens. This lack of publications makes Latino outreach a challenging effort for libraries. This book seeks to change the anticipated amount of library literature focusing on Latino teens.

Libraries are conduits of information—teens need information to finish high school and prepare for college. Some issues that come up when serving Latino teens truly and honestly do not have answers. So why bring them up? Because it allows us to forecast possible scenarios and consider options and plan future services. Library services have different incarnations and should not be seen as uniform or the recommendations as the official "right" way.

In the following chapter we review the multi-faceted process of purchasing items so that you may have a responsive and relevant collection for Latino teens.

References

Advertising Age. 2009. *2009 Hispanic fact pack*. http://adage.com/hispanic/ [accessed March 18, 2012].

Akst, Daniel. 2010. Apple's tablet and the future of literature. *Los Angeles Times*, January 24, A28 (1).

Becker, Samantha, Michael D. Crandall, Karen E. Fisher, Bo Kinney, Carol Landry, and Anita Rocha. 2010. *Opportunity for all: How the American public benefits from Internet access at U.S. libraries* (IMLS-2010-RES-01). Washington, D.C.: Institute of Museum and Library Services.

Collins, Jim. 2001. *Good to great: Why some companies make the leap . . . and others don't*. New York: HarperCollins.

Dubberly Garcia Associates, Inc. 2008. *The Las Vegas–Clark County Library District. Strategic service plan for FY 2008–2011*. Atlanta, GA.

Estudio AMIPCI. 2010. *2009 Sobre hábitos de los usuaros de Internet en México*. Monterrey, N.L.: Estudio AMIPCI .

Garcia, June, and Susan Kent. 2009. The challenge of change. Report to the mayor's task force on the revitalization and future of the Chattanooga-Hamilton County Bicentennial Library. www.chattanooga.gov [accessed March 18, 2012].

Grossman, Anna Jane. 2009. *Obsolete: An encyclopedia of once-common things passing us by*. New York: Abrams.

In New Jersey, text alerts for library programs. 2009. *Library Hotline* 38, no. 30 (August 3): 6–7.

Knight Commission on the Information Needs of Communities in a Democracy. 2009. *Informing communities: Sustaining democracy in the digital age*. Washington, D.C.: The Aspen Institute..

Lyons, Daniel. Jeff Bezos. 2010. *Newsweek*, January 4, 85–87.

Oldenburg, Ray. 1999. *The great good place*. New York: Marlowe & Company.

Packaged Facts. 2005. *The U.S. Hispanic market*. 6th edition. New York.

Powers, William. 2010. *Hamlet's blackberry: A practical philosophy for building a good life in the digital age*. New York: HarperCollins.

Southern Education Foundation, Inc. 2010. *A New diverse majority: Students of color in the South's public schools*. Atlanta, 13. www.southerneducation.org [accessed March 18, 2012].

5

Collection Development

Since 2002, reading has increased at the sharpest rate (+20 percent) among Hispanic Americans, though they still read literature at a lower rate than every other ethnic/racial group.

—National Endowment for the Arts, *Reading on the Rise: A Chapter in American Literacy*

It is customary for librarians to ask teens what they are interested in reading, with the intent of purchasing those items so that teens might frequent the library more regularly. Asking teens for their input is just part of the process of serving them well. This does not ensure that you will be able to act with the Latino teen's best interest in mind. Including some Latino teens in your information-gathering process will provide some leads but will not necessarily represent your entire Latino teen population. This may sound confusing and contradictory, but read on and you'll better understand.

The following recommendations are intended to guide librarians through the collection development maze. They are meant as a starting point rather than a definitive list. The key is that your teen collection be given a separate section of the library, instead of adjacent to or interfiled with adults' or children's materials.

Which One Is It—English or Spanish?

One question I often hear concerns whether materials for Latino teens should be in Spanish or English. My response is, it depends. For example, the *2008 Latinos and Public Library Perceptions* commissioned by Web-Junction found that "friendly staff service was a strong predictor of library visits, even stronger than access to Spanish Language materials" (Flores and Pachon 2008). The same report also found that "Latinos reported somewhat more satisfaction with English materials than Spanish materials" (Flores and Pachon 2008).

Consider a popular current series—The Twilight Saga. *Twilight* in English is generally more relevant to Latino teens than *Crespúsculo*, its Spanish version. If *Crespúsculo* is checked out, you can be sure that one of two things are occurring: 1) Latino teens that predominantly speak Spanish are checking it out; and/or 2) the parents of Latino teens that happen to be first generation are checking them out. Don't assume that the majority of Latino teens are reading the Spanish version, because they probably are not.

Cross-Promote Book Titles

For her article *What Do Teens Want?*, Carol Fitzgerald polled teens on what they had been reading. One of the discoveries was that "since teens read adult titles in significant numbers, it would make sense for adult publishers to reach out to them and for booksellers and librarians to cross promote titles" (2009, 23). This article goes into some detail regarding teens' buying and reading decisions. Based on her survey results, Fitzgerald was able to compile a list of the top read genres. Surprisingly, and interestingly, these are the top five "what they read" genres: Fiction, Series, Romances, Fantasy, and Adventure—all in English.

Libraries should forecast and be leaders in providing relevant materials to teens. English is the language of today and of the future. When asked if soap operas or other Spanish program shows may be trendy among young, integrated Latinos, "Antonio Mejias, entertainment editor at Los Angeles' *La Opinión*, the largest Spanish-language newspaper in the U.S., is skeptical. 'Yes, there will always be an audience for Spanish-language TV for immigrants, but I am very doubtful that there is an audience for Spanish content among long-term immigrants and those born here. Young Hispanics are quick to make the move to higher-quality English language programming'" (Martinez and Smith 2009, 60). That is why the above list of genres is being read in record numbers—the quality of the story is much better and relevant than that of a comparable Spanish book.

Sales representatives of major library distributors have seen a shift in language preference from Spanish to bilingual to English materials, which sometimes puzzles them, because everyone is under the impression that Latino teens in general would seek Spanish first—or the belief that reading in your native language is best. There are pros and cons to both positions. The current professional approach is neither functional nor validated sufficiently by library or reading research.

The most recent case study conducted by the Tomás Rivera Policy Institute for WebJunction confirmed that "although it may appear that a strong correlation exists because library visits influence English fluency, our regression findings suggest that satisfaction with English materials is more pivotal in increasing visits than satisfaction with Spanish materials" (Flores and Pachon 2008, 7). Stephen D. Krashen, a linguist and educational researcher focusing on second language acquisition has discovered that "free reading in the first language may mean more reading, and hence more literacy development, in the second language" (2004).

During the 2010 Public Library Association (PLA) Annual Conference in Portland, Oregon, the workshop "Multicultural Programming: Sharing Similarities and Celebrating Differences" offered some guidelines for evaluating children's books featuring Latinos. Even though these guidelines are intended for children's materials, they may be easily transferred to teen materials. Some of their key instructions were:

- Examine the personal traits of the character;

- Examine the roles of various characters;

- Examine and identify cultural stereotypes;

- Examine the diversity of representation in text and illustrations; and

- Examine the experience of the author or illustrator.

In the Las Vegas-Clark County Library District, Nevada, 25 percent of the population is of Latino heritage. Teens compromise a decent share of this percentage. Some alarming statistics as of this writing are that Southern Nevada, specifically Las Vegas, the entertainment capital of the world, is the most stressful city in the country; has the second worst divorce rate; has high dropout rates; runs the most red lights; has the highest unemployment rate in the country, 14 percent; and the list goes on and on. One promising development is that the library's Young Adult circulation statistics show a gradual increase between 2009 and 2010.

Must Have Core Collection Points

Librarians should allocate their collections in light of teen needs and wants, whatever they may be, so long as they are aligned with the libraries' strategic plan or preferred service priorities. I am a firm believer in having three types of print sections (not including electronic media). The three teen print service points that have proven successful when building or enhancing collections are: 1) classics; 2) middle and high school reading list titles; and 3) nontraditional print materials, such as magazines and graphic novels that appeal to teens. Some of the popular titles that have proven to be relevant with teens may be found within your general collection and do not necessary need a separate space. When a teen zone collection is properly marked with signage, teens will move in that direction. Once there, they will browse and discover on their own terms what this section has to offer. Chances are that they will give it a try before giving up on the quality and quantity of the collection found in this teen zone. The importance of the three print service points is that they support the teen's educational experience. For the most part, English courses have a list of classics that are recommended. This classics section should be arranged by author, and the format should be paperback. I say paperback because my experience has shown they will definitely get much use and you will have a good return on your investment per book.

Most middle and high schools have reading lists by grade level that are either mandatory or recommended reading. In order to facilitate the process of teens finding the books that they are looking for in an efficient and effective manner when they set foot in the library, why not cater to them by having a collection that you know will be used? The process of starting and maintaining this section is quite simple. You collect as many area school lists as possible, purchase what your budget allows, and then dedicate a section with signage. Teens should be able to find the section without asking for assistance from the library staff. The same holds true for the collection point of graphic novels and magazines. When clearly displayed and found within the realm of the teen section, these titles will contribute to the overall effectiveness of that collection. Don't be surprised if you see adults hovering in this section, as they, too, enjoy reading graphic novels. And remember, each of these three sections should be accompanied with chairs and tables for leisure reading and studying.

Space Allocation for Latino Teen Materials

I have heard claims that having the Spanish-language collection up front and accessible makes it inviting for the Spanish-speaking community. Without short- or long-term statistics from public libraries to trace its effectiveness this practice has yet to be substantiated. On the other hand, placing Spanish-language materials at the front of the library deprives Spanish speakers of the entire library collection, which might be of interest to them, including books in English. This oft-repeated recommendation has not yet proven to be a successful strategy. Hypothetically speaking, it carries absolutely no merit whatsoever.

When building your collection for Latino teens, consider these three factors:

- Whether your Latino teen users are first, second, or third generation;

- What subject matters are of interest to them, and

- Whether or not to purchase books in Spanish.

With so many genres and books currently available, your selection options are almost endless. Of course, there is no guarantee your teens will prefer one genre over the other. Consider street fiction (or urban literature). This genre is seemingly highly popular with the African American community, but does that appeal transfer to the Latino community? Three street fiction titles come to mind that may, or may not, relate to Latino teens. They are *The Devil's Mambo* by Jerry Rodriguez (Kensington Books 2007), *Forever My Lady* by Jeff Rivera (Warner Books 2007), and *Divas Don't Yield* by Sofia Quintera (Ballantine 2006). While some teens opt for this type of reading, others do not. Actually, there is no direct correlation between street lit and reading habits of Latino teens, which makes the librarian's task even more difficult.

You may recall some controversy described in the professional literature in recent years over public libraries including fotonovelas in their collections. Fotonovelas are more pictorial than street or urban fiction, but the essence and scope remains the same. Latino teens are no strangers to this genre; but in my experience, most have no interest in it. Even the risqué images portrayed in many of these fotonovelas did not spark interest or encourage many Latino teens to read them. What usually happens is that they are very popular and widely read in a person's native country. They are easy books to read, plus the pictures by themselves almost tell the entire story. While fotonovelas resonate mainly with Latinos of all ages in their native country, librarians in the States make the erroneous assumption that because they are read back home they will be read in the States. While Latino teens either used to read or know about them, they are not big attention grabbers in the States because they are seen as old-fashioned; and, Latino teens want to read what is more prevalent with the general teen population, which does not include fotonovelas.

What you purchase is predicated on who you are serving. One book that resonates with many male teens from varied backgrounds is *Finding Our Way* by René Saldaña, Jr. This book consists of 11 short stories. Note that this book was not translated to Spanish. The question that many publishers face is whether certain books will generate sales when translated. With the current trend of Latino teen demographics toward speaking English and many budgetary constraints libraries are facing, buying books in Spanish may not be a sound investment. Talk to a major book vendor who sells to public schools, and they will confirm that Latino teens in general prefer English-language materials. A well-suited and completely unused Spanish collection in the young adult or teen's section serves no one, and does not represent good stewardship of taxpayers' monies. Consider the following example of how one book did not have a return on investment.

Lengua Fresca

Let's assess our acumen regarding Latino literature as it relates to circulation. Consider Harold Augenbraum's *Lengua Fresca: Latino Writings on the Edge*. This book is a compilation of fiction and nonfiction from well-known to up-and-coming authors. The book cover features a nice illustration of a car with hydraulics. The Las Vegas-Clark County Library District, at which I am happily employed, purchased six copies of this book, with the record being created in December 2006. The copies were assigned to the libraries with dense Latino communities. This book received good reviews, and its description sounds enticing. With this limited information, what is your hunch regarding its circulation? Do you believe that it would circulate a great deal or collect dust? Over the course of three years (2007–2009) all six copies combined only circulated a grand total of 18 times. That equals one circ per year. You would think that the front cover would be enough to make it circulate even more. You would think that more people would be interested in these types of stories. So why is it that this particular book did not fare so well in circulation? Is literature on its last leg? Could it be that Latino literature is not relevant? Did the Spanish-language title put off young readers? We don't know for sure. What we do know is that some titles will be successful while others will not, so it's important not to make assumptions.

The informational and recreational reading needs and wants of Latino teens vary tremendously. Latino teens' taste in books, magazines, TV shows, music, and movies range from cultural to mainstream. The following examples demonstrate the degree and variety of topics that Latino teens are interested in and offer you a glimpse of the many types of items they will read, listen to, and view.

Teen Books

It's simple to create a bibliography of teen books, post them, and hope that teens will review the list and read them. If only it were this simple. Unfortunately, the secret to getting teens to read is much more complex, because there are many contributing factors that encourage teens to read or discourage them from reading. It is a proven fact that teens enjoy reading books of all genres in all age groups. For example, you might say that Latino teens, like other teens, often gravitate toward best sellers and pop culture titles, but also enjoy titles with characters they can identify with. The mystery of being successful is simply that if teens find one book that changes their mind about the art of reading, they will pick up more books knowing that they contain a wealth of stories that they might enjoy. More importantly, they will thrive in knowing that each reading experience is different and subject to many surprises. Given the personal nature of reading, it is extremely hard to predict what book will capture a Latino teen's attention, so we need to offer a broad selection. Below you will find a list of fiction and nonfiction titles that have had some influence on the reading habits of teens in general, which, for the most part, transcends to Latino teens.

- FICTION

  Twilight by Stephanie Meyers (Little, Brown 2006).

  The Alphabet of Manliness by Maddox (Kensington Publishing 2009).

  Bless Me Ultima by Rudolfo Anaya (Grand Central Publishing 1994).

  Chicano by Richard Vasquez (HarperCollins 2005).

  Naruto by Masashi Kishimoto (VIZ Media LLC; series).

  Bleach by Tite Kubo (VIZ Media LLC; series).

  Call Me Maria by Judith Cofer Ortiz (Scholastic 2006).

  Diario de Greg by Jeff Kinney (Lectorum Publications; series).

  Before We Were Free by Julia Alvarez (Random House 2004).

  Mexican Whiteboy by Matt de la Peña (Random House 2008).

  Dark Dude by Oscar Hijuelos (Atheneum 2008).

  Silvertongue by Charlie Fletcher (Hyperion 2009).

  Hidden Voices by Pat Lowery Collins (Candlewick Press 2009).

- NONFICTION

    The Good Neighbors by Holly Black (Scholastic; series).

    Good Behavior: A Memoir by Nathan Henry (Bloomsbury USA 2010).

    Fit Home Team by Laura Posada and Jorge Posada (Atria Books 2009).

Magazines

"In 2006, Hispanic/Latino teens constituted 20% (an estimated 6.3 million) of the U.S. teen population," according to the Magazine Publishers of America (2006). They tend to text more than the general population and start most fads that become mainstream. Having magazines that they take pleasure in will draw them into your library. Some trendy publications with brief annotations provided by bn.com (the Barnes & Noble Web site) are:

Lowrider—the premiere magazine for the lowrider enthusiast! This one-of-a-kind publication is packed with the best lowrider vehicles in the world. Every issue brings you showcases of the most incredible lowriders, exciting show coverage, world-record hops, wild dancers, cultural insights, technical how-to's and much more. Whether you're into traditional, bombs, euros, bikes or models, this magazine has something to excite or inspire you. Only *Lowrider* brings you culture, pride, artistry, and style!

Import Tuner—The baddest cars and the entire tech you need— *Import Tuner* is the magazine for the entry-level enthusiast. Each monthly issue helps readers make smarter purchases with product tests, dyno charts, and no-nonsense tech articles.

Truckin'—*Truckin'* magazine is the custom truck enthusiasts' bible! Each month it features road tests, product features, and pictorials. How-to articles address performance and technical aspects of custom trucks, superchargers, graphics, accessories, and more.

Sports Illustrated—*Sports Illustrated* is packed with complete coverage of all your favorite sports, including the World Series, the Super Bowl, the NBA Championship, the Final Four, the Olympics, and more.

Seventeen—*Seventeen* is the world's most popular magazine for today's young woman. Every issue brings you everything you need to know—about everything that's important to you. Seventeen covers everything from high school to Hollywood, including guys, clothes, friendships, music, school, movies, dating, and much more!

Latina—*Latina* magazine is a bilingual lifestyle publication for successful acculturated Hispanic women in the United States. *Latina* features the real women inspiring change in their communities, their families, and their jobs, and also covers fashion, beauty, culture, food, celebrity profiles and interviews, and much more!

Teen Vogue—*Teen Vogue* is a fashion magazine for teenagers who are passionate about style, the fashion industry, beauty, health, and entertainment news. *Teen Vogue* represents the best in teen fashion through gorgeous photography, world-class styling, and access to the fashion industry's brightest stars.

People en Español—*People en Español* features an exciting mix of Hispanic and mainstream entertainment coverage, compelling human-interest stories and the best in fashion and beauty. Only *People en Español* brings you the latest talk from Tinseltown, including gotta-get-it gossip, hip-hot styles of the stars, and sizzling celebrity profiles.

Ultimate MMA—*Ultimate MMA* magazine covers the world of mixed martial arts (MMA) and Ultimate Fighting Championships, including interviews with the biggest names in the sport, instructional features, product reviews, nutritional advice, and up-close-and-personal profiles of up-and-coming fighters and ring girls.

A Magazine Publishers of America report titled *Hispanic/Latino Market Profile* (2006) found some interesting statistics as to the magazine reading habits of Latino teens. Some of the data reveal that magazines are essential materials for teens, and should be part of teen zone service points. Magazines have an advantage over books in that they offer simple articles or short narratives, often illustrated with color photos that do not take too much time away from the teen's busy schedule.

When building your teen magazine collection, consider the following information from the *Hispanic/Latino Market Profile*:

- Hispanic/Latino teens bring great benefits to magazine advertisers: they have a strong affinity for brand names and tend to be more loyal and influential than non-Hispanic/Latino teens across several product categories;

- Eighty percent of Hispanic/Latino teens are magazine readers, a rate that is similar to that of U.S. teens as a whole (78 percent); and

- Hispanic/Latino teen magazine readers have a median of $85.64 in spending money per month, not including spending money from a job—7.4 percent higher than the median of $79.72 per month for all U.S. teens.

Music

If you have ever seen a group of teens gathered together, you probably noticed that most of them have earbuds or headphone sets of some sort to listen to their favorite music. If they own a vehicle, chances are that they have loud car stereos with monster speakers. Latino teens are not that much different from other teens. You will likely hear them play any of these musical groups:

- Linkin Park

- Bullet for My Valentine

- Nelly Furtado

- Gamblers Mark

- Los Mocosos

- Jennifer Lopez

- Shakira

- Mr. Capone-E

- Lil Rob

- Luis Miguel

- Lupillo Rivera

- Los Tigres Del Norte

The Recording Industry Association of America (RIAA) shares figures regarding musical preferences by genre. From their *2008 Consumer Profile*, the following is a breakdown of how three popular music genres did in 2008. They are:

- Rock = 31.8 percent

- Rap/Hip-hop = 10.7 percent

- R&B/Urban = 10.2% percent

In addition, the RIAA also released the *2008 RIAA Year-End Shipment Statistics for Latin Music*. The information that follows is based on manufacturers' unit shipments. Genre Breakout (percent based on suggested list price):

- Regional Mexican/Tejano = 62 percent
- Pop/Rock = 24 percent
- Tropical = 9 percent
- Urban = 5 percent

TV Shows

Television viewing is widespread throughout out the country, and Latinos teens are no exception. If conventional wisdom were to be true, you would notice higher viewership among Latino teens of shows that are Latino or Spanish based. However, current trends show that Latino teens do not fit that mold. Latino teens more often than not are watching mainstream shows enjoyed by viewers from all walks of life. If you study the many titles of these most watched shows, they are not culturally based nor do they target Latino teens, except perhaps for *The George Lopez Show*. *Friday Night Smackdown* is even getting into the business of introducing Latino wrestlers, such as Rey Misterio and Alberto Del Rio, to their burgeoning sport as they understand that a big part of their viewership are people of Latino heritage. This is a good time to reinforce the concept that speaking the culture is equally if not more important than speaking the language. Latino teens are embracing shows that were once viewed only by the English-dominant community. What do these shows have that appeal to Latino teens or community? Read the following quotes from Wikipedia to observe what is appealing about them. The answers might not be that obvious.

> Super Bowl—The Super Bowl is the championship game of the National Football League (NFL), the highest level of professional American football in the United States, culminating a season that begins in the late summer of the previous calendar year.

> American Idol—*American Idol* is a reality television competition to find new solo singing talent. The program aims to discover the best singer in the country where the winner is determined by the viewers.

Friday Night Smackdown—*WWE SmackDown* is a professional wrestling television program for World Wrestling Entertainment (WWE). As of 2010 it airs on Syfy in the United States as *WWE Friday Night SmackDown*.

Ugly Betty— Betty Suarez is a 22-year-old Mexican American woman from Queens, New York who is sorely lacking in fashion sense. She is known to be courageous, good-hearted, and slightly naive. She is abruptly thrust into a different world when she lands a job at *Mode*, a trendy high fashion magazine based in Manhattan that is part of the publishing empire of the wealthy Bradford Meade.

Heroes—The series tells the stories of ordinary people who discover superhuman abilities, and how these abilities take effect in the characters' lives. The series emulates the aesthetic style and storytelling of American comic books, using short, multi-episode story arcs that build upon a larger, more encompassing arc.

Prison Break—The series revolves around two brothers; one has been sentenced to death for a crime he did not commit, and the other devises an elaborate plan to help his brother escape prison.

Other popular shows with teens are:

Reno 911—had a Latino actor playing Deputy James Garcia.

UFC—has a great deal of Latino fighters, including Cain Velasquez.

WWE—stars from *Sin Caras* and other personalities.

There is a site that highlights what TV shows have been made into DVDs. Point your browser to http://www.tvshowsondvd.com/ for more information. Also, check websites such as http://bestsellers.about.com/ or http://www.ndtv.com/reading-room/booksmovies.asp to find out which books have made into movies, which are likely to be popular with Latino teens. A simple Google search will provide you with many more results.

Movies

There is a direct correlation between seeing a good number of movies and reading, according to Stephen K. Krashen in *The Power of Reading* (2004). It could be that moviegoers are more likely to have a print-rich environment and practice free voluntary reading, or it could be that movies engender a love of story or vice versa.

In any case, movies encourage young adults to appreciate reading and open their eyes to the pleasures of reading. Since many books are made into movies, this trend will continue to assist the publishing and library industries in promoting books. Below you will find some movies that are currently popular with Latino teens:

> *My Family*—starred some of the biggest names in Latino cinema.
>
> *Twilight*—what Latina would not like this love story?
>
> *High School Musical*—produced by Kenny Ortega.
>
> *Fast and Furious*—featured Michelle Rodriguez.

The *Movie Attendance Study* issued by the Motion Picture Association of America (MPAA) studies, among other things, the way Latinos view movies. Evidently, Latinos are watching more movies than ever before. If the hypothesis that movie watching promotes reading holds true, Latinos' reading habits will most definitely increase. Some of the major findings from the study are:

- Hispanic and Other moviegoers lead the way;

- Hispanic and Other moviegoers continue to see more movies per person than Caucasian moviegoers, though Caucasians still represent the majority of all moviegoers with 65 percent of views;

- Hispanics went to more movies in 2007;

- With 8 percent more Hispanic moviegoers than in 2006, this group was responsible for buying 297 million tickets (up 24 percent) and 10.8 tickets per person (up 17 percent) in 2007;

- Teens and the college-aged still dominate as most frequent moviegoers. There were 48 million teen and college-aged moviegoers; and

- Younger moviegoers go the most often.

- Moviegoers 12–24 years old represent 41 percent of all those who go to the theater at least once a month. Among all teens, 43 percent of frequent moviegoers are 16 or 17, up from only 35 percent in 2006 (MPAA 2007).

Online Booklists

If you are new to identifying books for your young adult or teen community, consider the lists below. They are an introduction to the type of genres that are read by teens in general. A quick disclaimer is that they sometimes do not break books down by most preferred by ethnicity and can make it difficult to identify good reads for Latino teens. In appendix D of this book, you will find a short list of graphic novels in Spanish, if you want to add them to your collection.

- Amazing Audiobooks for Young Adults. http://www.ala.org/yalsa/audiobooks [accessed March 18, 2012].

  Presents audiobooks released within the past two years that appeal to teens.

- Best Books for Young Adults. http://www.ala.org/yalsa/booklists/bbya [accessed on March 18, 2012].

  Compiles the current year's books with proven or potential appeal to teens.

- Fabulous Films for Young Adults. http://www.ala.org/yalsa/fabfilms [accessed on March 18, 2012].

  Presents select films on a chosen theme especially significant to young adults from those currently available for purchase.

- Great Graphic Novels for Teens. http://www.ala.org/yalsa/ggnt [accessed on March 18, 2012].

    Offers recommended graphic novels that have teen appeal; annual list.

- Outstanding Books for the College Bound. http://www.ala.org/yalsa/booklists/obcb [accessed on March 18, 2012].

    Provides reading recommendations to students who plan to continue their education beyond high school. Updated every five years, this comprehensive list was most recently released in 2009.

- Popular Paperbacks for Young Adults. http://www.ala.org/yalsa/booklists/poppaper [accessed on March 18, 2012].

    Encourages young adults to read for pleasure by presenting them with popular or topical books with teen appeal, built around up to four themes.

- Quick Picks for Reluctant Young Adult Readers. http://www.ala.org/yalsa/booklists/quickpicks [accessed on March 18, 2012].

    Suggests items for recreational reading that have wide appeal to teens who, for whatever reason, do not like to read.

- Teens' Top Ten. http://www.ala.org/yalsa/teenstopten [accessed on March 18, 2012].

    Allows teens to choose their ten favorite books from a list of current titles nominated by teen book groups. Nominations are listed in April. Teens vote for their favorite books each Teen Read Week. The votes are tallied and the list is available every October.

- Cozi. http://www.cozi.com/ [accessed on March 18, 2012].

    While this site has no direct correlation with books and reading, it does highlight the many online resources that are available to parents and librarians and how they may keep abreast of the many extracurricular activities that teens are involved in and how to determine their whereabouts. This site has been included as we librarians need to periodically shift away from library-oriented sites and focus on what may help Latino teens to be open and share with their parents.

    Cozi is a **FREE online organizer** that helps you manage the **family calendar**, organize your **shopping lists** and **to-do list**, and capture favorite memories in a **family journal**—all in one spot. Especially designed for busy moms and dads, Cozi is accessible from any computer or mobile phone.

Purchasing materials for today's users is no easy task. There are many contributing factors that make this a daunting experience. Don't fall subject to the Spanish-language misconception. Your Latino teen population might not be interested in Spanish-language material. All attempts to advance the Spanish-language collection will be met with disappointing outcomes. Instead, follow some of these best practices or simply poll Latino teens, and you will gain firsthand opinions as to what they value and prefer.

In the following chapter we review another essential benefit to serving Latino teens. You will be introduced to exciting best practices that will speed up your understanding and awareness of and improve your presence with Latino teens. Our discussion leads us to the focal purpose of rendering programs that are aligned with Latino teens.

References

Fitzgerald, Carol. 2009. What do teens want? *Publishers Weekly*, October 26, 23.

Flores, Edward, and Harry Pachon. 2008. *Latinos and public library perceptions*. Ontario, CA: Tomás Rivera Policy Institute.

Krashen, Stephen D. 2004. *The power of reading*. Westport, CT: Libraries Unlimited.

Krashen, Stephen D. 1996. *Under attack: The case against bilingual education*. Culver City, CA: Language Education Associates.

Magazine Publishers of America. 2004. *Hispanic/Latino market profile*. www.magazine.org/marketprofiles, 12 [accessed March 18, 2012].

Magazine Publishers of America. 2006. *Hispanic/Latino market profile*. Mediamark Research Inc. www.mediamark.com [accessed March 18, 2012].

Martinez, Andres, and Faith Smith. 2009. Switching channels. *Poder Enterprise Magazine* 69 (November): 60.

Motion Picture Association of America. 2007. *Movie attendance study*. http://www.mpaa.org/movieattendancestudy.pdf [accessed March 18, 2012] .

National Endowment for the Arts. 2009. *Reading on the rise: A chapter in American literacy*. Washington D.C.: NEA.

Recording Industry Association of America. 2008. *2008 consumer profile*. (cited July 21, 2009). www.riaa.com [accessed March 18, 2012].

Recording Industry Association of America. 2008. *2008 RIAA year-end shipment statistics for Latin music*. www.riaa.com. [accessed March 18, 2012].

6

Programs

You may think you know Hispanic teens . . .
but they are more than you think.

—*Nuestro Futuro: Hispanic Teens in Their Own Words*

Securing a captive audience for most library programs may seem to be a relatively effortless task. A large number of your returning families with children are aware of upcoming events. Adults on the other hand may or may not find the programming of their choice but are willing to visit other places for their needs and wants. However, many librarians seem uncomfortable or even distraught when contemplating or discussing programs for teens—and rightfully so. The diversity of teen needs and wants can be overwhelming. The library profession can't group all teens together or treat them completely separately during the programming development phase. And now we have to factor in the needs and wants of Latino teens, which means you have more than what you initially bargained for.

Seattle Public Library Community Survey Summary

One of the most encouraging documents about the library's strategic planning process comes from the Seattle Public Library in association with

Berk & Associates (2010). The Seattle Public Library Community Survey Summary highlighted respondents' preferences. Three themes that surfaced that are teen programming related were:

- Older respondents were generally more interested in staff assistance than younger respondents, with 41 percent of respondents 65 and older selecting staff help compared to 12% percent of teens (ages 15–19);

- Forty-five percent of respondents identified literary events (such as author readings and book talks) as a preferred programming option, followed closely by activities and education programs for teens and children, with 44 percent of respondents; and

- Teens preferred weekend afternoons to weekday evenings, while respondents age 65 and older preferred weekday evenings followed by weekday afternoons.

There are many great programs throughout the country doing exemplary jobs of reaching out to teens in general. There are far fewer of these best practices as they pertain to Latino teens. The ones that have been included here are general in scope and are both educational and recreational but offer prospects for connectedness as they deal with concerned staff. For too long, Latinos (and Latino teens) have been an afterthought. If you would like to speed up the process of working closely with them, you may need to conduct surveys to get to the root of their exact needs and wants. In the meantime you have to rely on the research that has been completed.

The Young Adult Library Services Association (YALSA) held a Young Adult Literature Symposium in November 2010 in Albuquerque, New Mexico, *Diversity, Literature & Teens: Beyond Good Intentions*, and the results were encouraging. The lineup of programs featured two workshops that commemorated Latinos and literature. They were "Celebramos Libros: Celebrating Latino Literature!" and "Talk the Walk: Learning New Book-talking Skills Designed to Reach a Variety of Diverse Teen Populations." Of course, this conference focused only on literature—not on other areas of service—didn't address some of the serious issues that Latino teens face, but it was a start.

The following programs, which range in scope and geographical locations, are but a few that may reverberate with Latino teens. Several trouble-free programs that should be encompassed by your strategic plan are listed below. These programs originate from the national level while extending to the state and local levels.

Leadership Initiatives

¡Excelencia in Education!
http://www.edexcelencia.org/ [accessed March 15, 2012]

> ¡Excelencia! is your information source for improving Latino
> student success. Excelencia in Education aims to accelerate
> higher education success for Latino students by providing data-
> driven analysis of the education status of Latino students and
> by promoting education policies and institutional practices that
> support their academic achievement.

In 2007, the State of Nevada Legislature created the Nevada Youth
Legislature. According to their Web site, http://www.leg.state.nv.us/lcb/
legal/NVYouthLegislature/, the Nevada Youth Legislature is composed of
21 high-school-age students who are selected from each of Nevada's senato-
rial districts. Each member of the Youth Legislature is appointed by a Nevada state senator with input from members of the Nevada State Assembly.
One of its most important tasks is to submit one legislative bill for enact-
ment which relates to matters within the scope of the Youth Legislature.
Knowing what you know of Nevada, what do you suppose their final proposal centered on? Their final proposal seeks to see the top age for compul-
sory school attendance in the state reduced from 18 to 16. According to the
student whose proposal won, if students do not want to attend school, they
are going to be a distraction to others, and that will hamper other students'
educational success. It is interesting to see what these bright kids thought
was the most pressing issue affecting their cohorts.

Employment Programs

Each year the Urban Libraries Council (ULC) recognizes programs or
initiatives that exemplify positive youth development and youth contributing to their communities. The ULC Highsmith Award of Excellence victors
are ULC members that serve midsized to large metropolitan urban areas of
100,000 or greater. The 2009 recipient was the District of Columbia Public
Library for their "Teens of Distinction Employment Program." According to
the ULC press release:

> the Teens of Distinction Employment Program provides part-time
> year-round youth and workforce development for D.C. residents
> between the ages of 16–19. With the goal of attracting more teens

as Library users, the program provides paid opportunities for
teens to assist with customer service, collections management
and special programming in the central library as well as all
neighborhood libraries (http://www.urbanlibraries.org/ [accessed
March 15, 2012])

A great source for understanding what life is like for Latino adolescents who were not born in the United States and how they adjusted to life
here may be found at the Latino Acculturation and Health Project at http://
www.unc.edu/~smokowsk/Main_Page.html [accessed March 15, 2012]. If you
are interested in reaching out to this segment of the Latino teen population, this
source covers the issues of importance to them that will enable you to tailor your
programs with their best interests in mind. What is noteworthy about this site is
its quest to "to see how Latino immigrant adolescents are similar or different
from Latino adolescents who were born in the United States."

An April 8, 2009, *School Library Journal* article described the results
of the 2009 Teen and Personal Finance survey. One very important statistic
is that 18 percent of teens lost a job due to the economy. This is a great opportunity for libraries to capitalize on by offering job preparedness workshops to educate teens about the importance of interviewing, budgeting, and
money management.

In other cases, you find educational organizations whose mission statement and purpose is to educate and empower teens through leadership development and civic participation.

One group that we can learn from that has a rapport with Latino teens
comes out of Las Vegas, Nevada. This is Latino Townhall, http://www
.latinotownhall.com/ [accessed March 15, 2012]. One of their programs that
can easily transfer to libraries is Life Coaching for Teens. A brief description
of that program follows:

Life Coaching for Teens: Building Confidence, Developing Character and Living Courageously!

Life Coaching for Teens was inspired by the state of Hispanic
community coupled with a willing heart to mentor Latino teens
in life and leadership development. This workbook provides life
and leadership principles for Latino youth so they can advance
and walk in success.

Building Confidence: This section introduces students to
foundational principles and concepts of identity and life purpose.
These two areas are critical for helping students know "who" they
are and "why" they exist; combined these concepts reveal one's

true significance in life. A person's "self-worth" is tied to their identity.

Developing Character: The middle section introduces students to the **Top 12 Virtues for Teens**, which are crucial for life success. When a student understands and adopts these 12 virtues they will learn to possess and master the characteristics to confront and overcome life's challenges, and walk in success.

Living Courageously: This final section delves into finding one's personal passion, which usually leads to one's life mission. We take students through a series of questions that probe and pinpoint their passion(s). Once passion is discovered, we work together to formulate a 5–10-year life plan to help teens move forward courageously. Cultivating and expressing courage throughout life is necessary to achieve great results and become a lifetime winner. Life Coaching for Teens is a great program because it is a lifelong learning initiative, which might not have been acquired at home, including households from all socio economic levels.

Day of the Dead Celebration

Think of this program primarily as an artistic event. Before I briefly highlight how this program should spark an interest with Latino teens, a short history lesson is appropriate. Day of the Dead, or Día de los Muertos, is a very popular occurrence in many Latin American countries. The purpose of observing Día de los Muertos is to observe and remember those who have died. Many customs are enacted to pay tribute to one's ancestors. Some of the most popular activities are to decorate grave sites with flowers and relax in the cemetery; create altars at one's house with the deceased's favorite food, drinks, and gifts in the form of offerings; and attend community events where societies and associations create elaborate altar displays. During these community events food and beverages are sold and enjoyed by all in the spirit of thinking of their deceased loved ones. While this might seem strange to non-Latinos, it is perfectly normal in the Latino community to have annual events, mainly during the last week of October and first week of November.

So how can such ritual be successful with Latino teens? Teens can work on one of their strengths within such a program. What is bound to happen during this learning process is that they will become more familiar with their cultural roots and the importance of celebration. Instead of spearheading or promoting this as a religious or cultural program, consider alternative approaches. Remember that Latino teens for the most part, especially if they are second, third, or fourth generation, don't know their grandparents that well. Regina Marchi writes that "Mexican Americans and other U.S. Latinos engage with the celebration for a variety of distinct reasons, including spiritual needs, artistic expression, political protest, community development, and commerce" (2009, 139). Cities with a substantial number of Latinos have established annual traditions around this holiday. Likewise, many libraries have been acknowledging this day and incorporating it into their program lineup. Remember that you do not have to do all of the legwork. Partner with a local cultural group and have them lead the project. You provide the space, and they will use their contacts to organize and put on a great quality program.

At first this may seem as a creepy concept—that is, building a display with pictures, food, artifacts, and skulls of dead people—but as you get into it, you will see the significance of this Latino celebration that will be enjoyed by a great majority of your library users.

Si Se Puede/Yes We Can!

According to Wikipedia, "Imperial County is a county located in the Imperial Valley, in the far southeast of the U.S. state of California, bordering both Arizona and Mexico. It is part of the El Centro, California Metropolitan Statistical Area which encompasses all of Imperial County. The population as of 2000 was 142,361." Mostly agricultural, Imperial County does not have the same lavish services and programs as large urban cities. However, in spite of the economic downturn and limited resources, some parents are still engaged in their teen's activities: image of Latina teen found on page 70 depicts a public performance of what may happen when both libraries and community members apply themselves to creating relatable programs. If you carefully study the picture of Latinas performing Zumba, you might notice that the public performance was conducted outdoors. No fancy meeting room or building. The dance was part of a fundraiser held by teens and parents, in which lowriders, motorcycles, and 18-wheelers were also on display. Think of it: if a low socioeconomic community can exercise, rehearse, and put on a public performance of this nature, why couldn't this happen within your respective service area?

How do you properly market these programs to Latino teens? The report "Between Two Worlds: How Young Latinos Come of Age in America" (Pew Hispanic Center 2009) explores the attitudes, values, social behaviors, family characteristics, economic well-being, educational attainment, and labor force outcomes of these young Latinos. Extrapolating from these findings, the author of "Hispanic Youth Treads a Difficult Path," comments on what Latino marketers are doing to reach Latino teens. One of the main points that librarians should understand and most importantly agree to is that the "relevance is not so much in the language but in the context of the advertising and whether they see themselves and their lifestyles reflected in the advertising" (Dolliver 2012) Even with this information in hand one has to be very thoughtful so as not to make the promotional piece too library centric. Analyze all the information within your possession and then address the culture of the teen; do not address the resources of the library and transfer them to teen needs and wants. It is prudent that librarians vigilantly examine their intentions and their impact, as this will be a defining moment when reaching out to Latino teens. Several cries that librarians use quite exhaustively are "read to succeed," "reading is important," "libraries offer homework assistance," and so forth. If we reflect on this practice, how do we know if we are connecting with them if we are not including their values and beliefs?

The following chapter leads us to the central facet of marketing and promoting to Latino teens.

References

Dolliver, Mark. 2012. Hispanic youth treads a difficult path. *Adweek*, January 3. http://www.brandweek.com [accessed March 18, 2012].

Marchi, Regina M. 2009. *Day of the Dead in the USA: The migration and transformation of a cultural phenomenon*. New Brunswick, NJ: Rutgers University Press.

Nuestro futuro: Hispanic teens in their own words. 2006. Redwood Shores, CA: Cheskin.

Pew Hispanic Center. 2009. *Between two worlds: How young Latinos come of age in America*. Washington, D.C.: Pew Hispanic Center.

The Seattle Public Library, and Berk & Associates. 2010. *The Seattle Public Library community survey summary*. Seattle, WA: Seattle Public Library, and Berk & Associates.

Teens feel the economic pinch in a big way, study says. 2009. *School Library Journal*, April 8. www.schoollibraryjournal.com [accessed March 18, 2012].

Wikipedia. Imperial County, California. http://en.wikipedia.org/wiki/Imperial_County,_California [accessed on March 15, 2012].

7

Marketing

Language itself isn't an issue; driving the importance of
meaningful and contextualized marketing efforts is the issue.

—*Nuestro Futuro: Hispanic Teens in Their Own Words*

The purpose of marketing, in its simplest terms, is to connect with customers. In this chapter we buck some of the conventional marketing wisdom and methods. As small or large agencies with a big undertaking, libraries have the dual purpose of building awareness and being relevant. There are two approaches that need to be considered. That is, should your marketing be customer based or library based? And is marketing one or two directional?

When we discuss marketing we have to incorporate some of the lessons learned in the Who are Latino Teens and Relationship Building chapters (1 and 3). One of the most bothersome questions of marketing for the first timer, novice, or even an experienced tenured library staff member is "How can we discuss or market something to a group we know absolutely nothing about?"

Start by reading books such as *Crash Course in Serving Spanish Speakers* by Salvador Avila (Libraries Unlimited 2008) to gain a foundational knowledge of the Latino community in general. Then enhance your understanding and awareness of who your target audience is—in this case Latino teens. Follow up by grasping what makes this community tick and not tick. By identifying their cultural characteristics, you, and other library advocates, will be better positioned to promote library services.

By incorporating some of the following techniques, borrowed from the private sector, you will likely gain many benefits. You will increase your knowledge in a short amount of time and decrease the time it takes to learn a new skill. But a word of caution must also be added. These marketing strategies are well suited for the private sector, and they require funding and promotion. Some portions can easily transfer to the public sector and yield high results; others are not so easy. After reviewing what big companies are doing to reach Latino teens, you can come away with some great ideas; but understand that you won't reach that level of success, as they have more funding, experts, and consulting firms at their disposal. What you can do is borrow the understanding of best practices. As stated in the opening quote, language itself isn't the issue; driving the importance of meaningful and contextualized marketing efforts is the issue.

Prominent Techniques

With the recent upsurge of advertising agencies and firms targeting the Latino community comes varied opinions about reaching this segment of the population. For the most part, these companies offer sound advice and recommendations. For a complete listing of these types of businesses, check out the Association of Hispanic Advertising Agencies at http://www.ahaa.org/.

Boden PR Hispanic is a public relations firm that focuses on developing and rolling out marketing to the U.S. Hispanic population. In a recent report, *Tips When Formulating U.S. Hispanic Youth Campaigns*, they offer four strategies:

1. Speak to them in their language;

2. Give them culturally relevant content, without stereotyping them;

3. Recognize reggaeton's rapidly growing popularity, but do not surround your entire marketing campaign around it; and

4. Look toward the future: give your marketing crossover appeal.

To be astute in marketing to Latino teens you have to be aware of the image you want to project. If you use Latino as a brand, some Latino teens might associate it with something that they are not interested in: something too ethnic for them.

A different example with the same objective is found in *The Guy-Friendly YA Library: Serving Male Teens*: "a simple photograph of teens (including teen boys) appearing in the paper and enjoying themselves at a library function will make the administration take notice more than any book talk or library display" (Welch 2007). Another approach is to include images of prominent individuals, not just celebrities. (See appendix E for a brief list of successful Latinos).

What is influencing today's Latino teens? Are you factoring in their varying levels of acculturation? How about their language use? Assimilation status? One successful strategy taking place in the charter school community that is easily transferable to the library section is illustrated in the next section.

Early Intervention

What many library directors, educators, principals, law enforcement officers, and community members need to understand is that early intervention may well be the best way of influencing a youngster's mind on any subject. Even though teens are subject to peer pressure and all of the issues that come with growing up, your outreach efforts should start early. For example, Dr. John and Wendi Hawk, administrators of Nevada State High School, a charter school whose vision is to lead the State of Nevada in transitioning high school students to college, are reaching out to middle schoolers. They wish to make an indelible impression of what attending a charter school entails. Librarians are already familiar with this concept; they know that if they don't encourage the love of reading and lifelong learning among third and fourth graders, they will have a harder time reaching these same students in later years.

Young adults will share certain characteristics as well as have distinct differences, and they have dual marketing preferences. They may seek the company of similar teens, or they may seek the company of young adults different from them, whether cultural, social, economic, psychological, technological, or sexual. While promoting or advertising to Latino teens, libraries need to employ market segmentation.

As previously stated, Latino teens share many characteristics; you can use this as a way to precisely target your prospects. By utilizing market segmentation, you also gain greater insight into the teens' cultural, social, economic, psychological, technological, and sexual wants and needs therefore allowing your library to become a customer-centric serving institution.

To be successful, you need to incorporate outreach into your daily tasks, duties, and responsibilities. Outreach is both institutionally and companionably good. Instead of being behind the desk carrying on routine tasks that will inevitably lead to carpal tunnel syndrome, sciatica, and several other ailments, outreach affords you the opportunity to work hand-in-hand with teens on their turf. You also have the opportunity to meet with representatives of other organizations and associations that share the same goals as yours. They may become networking sources in identifying and advancing library services through their contacts and knowledge of the community.

This kind of outreach entails working outside the library. As already shown in previous chapters, Latino teens use the library the least for Internet access, are the quickest to learn about mobile Web technology, and are gradually gaining ground with the general population in reading. If we want to truly be successful we should be joining forces with Safekey-type services, Boys & Girls Clubs, and any place where teens congregate to learn more about their needs. Then we can either partner with organizations and associations or do our best effort to offer similar services.

Reaching Latino Teens

In 2006, one of the most noteworthy marketing agencies for Hispanics, Cheskin, revealed in their report *Nuestro Future: Hispanic Teens in Their Own Words,* three significant findings. Besides frequenting the typical teen places, from the Internet and mainstream TV to the mall and the movie theater, Hispanic teens share these characteristics:

- Despite having more family activities than the typical teen, Hispanic teens are also drawn to "where the action is." Hispanic teens enjoy "teen" activities— hanging around with friends at home, going out to eat, and going to the movies. They love to dance, which is as much an expression of culture as of their optimism;

- They are on MySpace.com in droves and access mostly English-language Web sites to chat via instant messaging (IM), download music, and conduct research. AOL, Google, and Yahoo are all used and are vying for their loyalty; and

- Predominantly, mainstream broadcast media are primary choices among bicultural Hispanic teens. Frequently cited shows and networks included MTV, VH1, BET, *American Idol, That 70's Show, The Simpsons*, and *Family Guy*.

I have found that although including big-name celebrities in flyers and promotional materials can be effective, having local notable people gets the same results. Teens understand who is delivering the message and easily make up their mind if this person is credible. For example, if you have a rapper known to have dropped out telling students or teens to stay in school, the teens are likely to immediately cancel that message out, as they know that that person does not have the credentials to say such comments. Now, if that remark came from a respected and educated local individual, such as a mayor or city council member, those same teens will know that it comes from a reputable source and that that leader has gone through the process. Whether the message is educational, political, or social, this principle holds true. If you decide to take this course of action, do so with care. Latino teens, like the general teen population, don't need to be told to stay in school. As a librarian, you have to be discreet with your tactics. If all you do is explain the benefits of possessing a library card and showcase in detail the library's services and programs, they will become uninterested. Instead, your presentation should be more of a discourse or dialogue, where the students do most of the talking. Allow teens to converse freely and verbalize what they want and need. Ask questions. Let them articulate their thoughts and processes in detail so that you may walk away knowing exactly what they need from the library.

Generation Ñ

Another authority in marketing to Latinos, Isabel M. Valdés, has coined a name for this group, defining them as Generation Ñ. Generation Ñ includes Latinos ages 10 to 19: transitioning tweens, teens, and young adults. More than their predecessors, they are generally bilingual and open to adapting to the American way of life. At the same time, they are proud of their Latino heritage, and do not want to lose their Hispanic identity.

Keep in mind that just because you are talking with teens does not necessarily mean that you are communicating with them. When you share information, you basically let teens know what you have to offer. Only if the teens actually digest and respond to your subject matter has your message been communicated and conveyed. That is why when speaking and/or engaging with teens, it is a good practice to repeat in the form of a question what you have covered. For example, during an assembly or gathering ask all the teens at once how many books may be checked out at one time. In addition to a library card, what else do you need to access computers? This simple exercise will make teens more knowledgeable as you interact rather than just lecture, something they are too familiar with and don't need more of.

Marketing versus Other Approaches

When reaching out to teens, the word "marketing" may not be the correct one to use. Connecting, involving, and interacting are what they need.

While this conversation of which term to use for your efforts may be decided by a library committee or roundtable, what we do know is that libraries will need to do more reaching out to Latino teens now and in the foreseeable future. The study *Latino Children: A Majority Are U.S.-Born Offspring of Immigrants* concludes that "The nation's 16 million Hispanic children will likely continue to be one of our fastest-growing child populations. The U.S. Census Bureau projects that the number of Hispanic children will rise to 24 million by 2025 (Census Bureau, 2008). The share of children who are of Latino origin is projected to rise to 29% in 2025 from 22% today" (Fry and Passel 2008, 1).

Pretend for a moment that you are trying to design services for teens, and your heat maps illustrate a prominent presence of Latino teens in your community. You'd like to explore a number of tactics targeting Latino teens within your service area, but you are not quite sure what the best way to go about it is. After all, when it comes to serving Latino teens, there are all sorts of conflicting opinions on how to best serve them. What you really need is a crystal ball that will share with you how to arrive at your destination in the quickest way possible. That is where these successful marketing tips may come in handy.

Some new groundbreaking research states that computer usage among low socioeconomic status Latino teens is low, while other research states that these same teens believe in the library. What is your ticket to relevancy? Serving Latino teens! Most are bilingual and bicultural, and they tend to embrace change with less frustration and hesitation, especially if they are part of Generation Z. Being bilingual and bicultural allows them to navigate quite successfully the best of both worlds and cultures. They can shift gears with ease and in a moment's notice and in almost any type of situation that works to their advantage.

As noted previously, Joey Rodgers, former president of the Urban Libraries Council, once said that libraries are in the library business; but libraries are also in the community business. If the marketing department and/ or librarian responsible for advertising the brand, services, and programs of the library are not familiar with Latinos, much less Latino teens, they might have some superficial or incorrect perceptions about this segment of the community. In a leading publication on diversity and business, Alma Morales Riojas writes that "one problem is that Latinos, regardless of their national origin, are falsely perceived as newly arrived immigrants who are poor, uneducated and lacking English skills" (2009, 38). As we have seen, nothing could be farther from the truth.

I am a firm believer that the burden of rendering relevant and responsive library services to Latino teens falls solely on the provider. It is your responsibility to ask questions on how you can best serve them. Do not rely on prior perceptions or past practices or on speculating about what they need. And remember, in order to reach tomorrow's teens, focus on Generation Z (which includes children born roughly between 2001 and 2010) who are entering the school system as we speak.

If you have ever attended a training session/workshop or read about reaching the Latino population, you have probably heard that word of mouth is a popular way of spreading a message. This practice may hold true for the adult community; you can consult with the Word of Mouth Marketing Association, http://womma.org/main/ for best practices in this area. For Latino teens, "word of mouth" looks more like texting and social networking, two completely different formats all together.

The Patron or You

Serving Latino teens, or the general population, may be considered a two-way street. Which of these two approaches carries more weight? Option 1 asserts that Latino teens should know about your existence and services. Option 2 avows that you, the library, should be well versed about the population that you are trying to reach. These two approaches are completely different and will yield different results as they both require different ploys and schemes. After reading the two options listed above, do you suppose that they require different ways of conveying messages or catching their attention? A library could make great strides toward knowing its community and at the same time fail to alert Latino teens about its existence.

Why is this concept so important? Jack Trout stresses that "it is not about knowing your customer. It's about your customer knowing about you" (Trout 2000). What makes Latino teens different is that the message is two directional, and if not handled correctly, it can have some detrimental effects. Some portions of the Latino community prefer direct communication that broadcasts and is informational. Another portion prefers to have dialogues with staff and others to become well versed in what the library is trying to accomplish. Unless the library profession masters the art of making sure that Latino teens can distinguish and grasp the fact that libraries are there to serve them, our approach of simply studying them isn't going to be successful.

Why is this important? As librarians, we are only cognizant of a small portion of the community at any given time. If you want teens wanting to know, recognize, and appreciate the library as a place, will your traditional tactics work? If your answer is I do not know, you will have to invest valuable time becoming aware of what may make Latino teens know more about the library. Don't be surprised to find out that it does not come from presentations or speeches on the importance of library services.

"Give teens what they want" is a commonly held principle when referring to Latino teen services. But when comparing them with non-Latino teens, you must also explore answers to questions rather than taking them at face value. For example, if you ask a male Latino teen, "Do you like to read?" the teen might say no. If you were to dig deeper you might discover that he does read the assigned school reading lists but doesn't necessarily like it. During this digging deep session, you might also learn that he is an avid graphic novel reader or spends a lot of time reading online, but because the teacher or school doesn't recognize this as official literature, the teen is under the false impression that this is not legitimate reading. Sometimes mandatory reading only accomplishes one thing: it discourages teens from reading. While required reading materials are important, teens may feel differently toward the subject matter and reading altogether.

When it comes to marketing, many of the old misconceptions have lingered on, while the target group has transformed, making any marketing efforts of no consequence. Audacious efforts have to be incorporated to better reach Latino teens, and many have failed.

According to the *Latinos in America* series by Soledad O'Brien, the state of being cool Latinos has been defined with the following words in both English and Spanish and in Spanish from different countries: *chévere*, *bacano*, cool, *padre*, and *bárbaro*. If you were to market to Latino teens, do you think that you would have used these types of words to make public your many services and programs? Whatever your answer is, you now see the complexity of campaigning and championing your services and programs to this diverse group.

Who Is Herculez Gomez?

Take a look at the life of Herculez Gomez. Mr. Gomez played for the U.S. soccer team during the 2010 World Cup that took place in South Africa. Even though the United States did quite well in the tournament, Mr. Gomez left an even more lasting impression on the world and among Latinos of all ages. Follow this link http://www.lvrj.com/sports/not-how-the-ball-usually-bounces-96864629.html, to read what makes Herculez Gomez noteworthy to Latino teens. The title of the news article is "Not How the Ball Usually Bounces." It highlights the struggles and tribulations that Herculez had to endure in order to make it to the U.S. Olympic soccer team. He stresses how he did not have the same opportunities to be involved in elite soccer leagues like other youths his age but still managed to take advantage of the opportunities that surfaced and was always waiting to open the door when opportunity knocked.

What is my point in sharing the example of this sports figure? When you market or more importantly speak to groups of Latino heritage, it is important to relay successful stories. Stress the successes of an individual, family, or company, and Latinos of all ages will be somewhat inspired. Once you have conveyed your message, ask the Latino community what characteristics are imperative or prerequisite to being successful. If you are trying to advance the library, you can mention the concept of a Print Rich Environment (PRE). The premise of a PRE is that literature or reading materials should be in the household at all times to model to the entire family that reading is valued and cherished. The reading material may be newspapers, magazines, a personal book collection, or the books that have been recently borrowed by the family. Over time you may inform your captive audience that this practice has proven successful because you instill the respect and importance of reading both leisurely and for educational reasons.

In conclusion, consider these four pointers that are the grounds for marketing to Latino teens. They are:

- Listen openly and carefully;

- Briefly and clearly explain things;

- Show manners and respect; and

- Spend quality time with Latino teens.

Simply adhering to these four directives with true dedication will demonstrate the library's strength of character and be a building block for making sure that as many Latino teens as possible are familiar with your many services and programs.

In Spanish *circulacion* means a flow of traffic, as opposed to the library meaning of checking items out. Would you use *circulacion* to refer to your circulation or customer services department after seeing this image? For your information, *salida*, which means to exit, is used in many Latin and South American countries to represent checking-out service points.

The following chapter will introduce you to exciting best practices that can speed up your understanding and awareness of and improve your presence with Latino teens. Our discussion leads us to parents as stakeholders and ambassadors when offering library services to Latino teens.

References

Avila, Salvador. 2008. *Crash Course in Serving Spanish-Speakers*. Santa Barbara, California: Libraries Unlimited.

Boden PR. *Tips when formulating U.S. Hispanic youth campaigns*. www.bodenpr.com [accessed March 15, 2012].

Cheskin. 2006. "Nuestro futuro: Hispanic teens in their own words." www.cheskin.com [accessed March 15, 2012].

Fry, Richard, and Jeffrey S. Passel. 2008. *Latino children: A majority are U.S.-born offspring of immigrants*. Washington, D.C.: Pew Hispanic Center.

O'Brien, Soledad. 2009. *Latino in America*. New York: Penguin.

Riojas, Alma Morales. 2009. Ushering in a new era for Latinos. *DiversityInc.*, September/October, 38.

Trout, Jack. 2000. *The power of simplicity: A management guide to cutting through the nonsense and doing things right*. New York: McGraw Hill.

Valdés, M. Isabel. 2008. *Hispanic customers for life: A fresh look at acculturation*. New York: Paramount Publishing, Inc.

Welch, Rollie James. 2007. *The guy-friendly YA library: Serving male teens*. Westport, CT: Libraries Unlimited.

8

Motivational Strategies

Good is the enemy of great

—Jim Collins, *Good to Great*

Now that you've become acquainted with all facets of serving Latino teens, there is one final aspect of service that you should consider—parents of Latino teens. Including parent participation in Latino teen services and programs is imperative to your success. This approach differs significantly from that of serving the general teen population; typical American parents, as a rule of thumb, allow their teens more liberty and freedom. There is a pronounced difference with first-generation parents who have second-generation teens. Since the first-generation parent is not all that familiar with the "system," they are not able to offer the best advice to their teen as they do not have the experience or knowledge to counsel or guide them. One example of this might be observed in the school system. The first-generation parent might not be familiar with the school curriculum and therefore not encourage their teenage children to enroll in advanced classes. Their lack of expertise places their kids at a disadvantage because the parent will not be able to persuade the school administration that more advanced classes are appropriate, especially in middle and high school.

Parent Involvement

Instead of just serving Latino teens, you have to make a presence with first-generation parents, who often happen to be Spanish-language speakers. Of course, second- and third-generation parents have a greater awareness of how American society works and understand how libraries fit in their every-day life. Since second- and third-generation parents have, hopefully, completed high school, they are aware of the basic requirements for graduation. They know that a simple high school diploma makes it easier to find a job, especially if the students are not college material. First-generation parents need to be more involved in the upbringing of their young adults. This will ultimately bring the best results.

This is where the library may come in and work with schools and social service providers to introduce services that parents and teens "might" not be familiar with. Remember, there is sufficient evidence that illustrates that, at least in Mexico, people do not visit libraries. According to an article that appeared in *El Universal*, survey results relating to habits and practices found that 43 percent do not know of a public library. If you are in a library system with a Spanish-speaking constituency, you have a great opportunity to create public value with them. This is probably the first compilation of motivational messages from today's top Spanish-language experts that you can employ to end our nation's library usage gap. In your quest to introduce and encourage the use of library services to Spanish-speakers, especially during these turbulent economic times, it is imperative that your library become a driving force in inspiring Spanish-speakers.

To facilitate the process of creating public value among Spanish-speakers, consider using the following strategies. You may feel that this is a change in direction from previous practices and is outside your comfort zone. All too many librarians pigeonhole themselves, believing that they cannot serve Spanish-speakers because they don't speak Spanish. In reality, they should be thrilled about the challenge—here is an opportunity to learn a new relevant skill set. Through these types of interactions Spanish-speakers will see that you have leadership qualities, which in turn will make you a trusted source.

Allow me to explain. During my tenure as community outreach librarian for the Las Vegas-Clark County Library District in Las Vegas, Nevada, when asked to speak to Spanish-speaking community and parent groups, each time the organizer would ask me to share motivational stories and leadership skills as part of my presentation. I noticed that during the course of these presentations, Spanish-speakers were avidly interested in this subject matter. Yes, they were also interested in hearing what the library had to offer, but they were paying more attention to how they might thrive and succeed in this country. That is because leadership is much more personal and emotional than a library sales pitch. Sharing motivational stories and talking about leadership will encourage Latinos to associate leadership with libraries. In my book *Crash Course in Serving Spanish-Speakers*, you can find profiles of some prominent Latinos to showcase as role models for Latino teens. Using these inspiring stories will gain you respect in the Latino community and allow you to be closer with Spanish-speakers.

But let's dig a little deeper and examine the underlying messages that Spanish-language motivational speakers use today and consider how libraries might apply them to their own messages.

Spanish-Language Motivational Speakers and Books

You are likely already familiar with such motivational speakers as Napoleon Hills, Zig Ziglar, Og Mandino, Robert T. Kiyosaki, and Dale Carnegie, to name a few. Most Spanish-language motivators use materials from these great speakers in their talks, presentations, and books. One of the major themes of Spanish-language motivators is *el exito*—success.

Camilo Cruz
www.camilocruz.com

In *Los genios no nacen ¡se hacen! Cómo programar tu mente para triunfar y ser feliz* (which loosely translates to: geniuses are not born, they are made, how to program your mind to succeed and be happy), Dr. Camilo Cruz shares 60 tips for being successful. Let's analyze one of his many messages:

> *Las personas que triunfan desean triunfar y eligen un camino que incluye definer claramente sus metas y se visualizan en posesión de estas. Saben que deben prepararse para triunfar; van tras sus metas con el firme propósito de lograrlas y no se detienen hasta conseguir aquello que les pertenece.* (Cruz 2003, 73)

In other words, people who succeed wish to succeed and elect a road that involves clearly defining their goals and visualizing possessing them. They know that they need to prepare themselves to achieve something; they go after their goals with a firm conviction of reaching them and do not stop until they earn what rightfully belongs to them.

Miguel Angel Cornejo
www.cornejoonline.com

One of the most established Spanish-language motivational figures is Mr. Cornejo. In *Únete a la excelencia* he discusses attributes necessary to design our future right here and now. They include:

1. *Superación: Plan de vida para triunfar;*
2. *Visión y misión: Un porqué vivir;*
3. *Trabajo: El valor del esfuerzo;*
4. *Honestidad: La gran diferencia;*
5. *Servicio: La magia de ser útil; and*
6. *Educación: La virtud de aprender* (Cornejo 1995, 100–103).

Translated to English:

1. Self improvement: Life plan in order to triumph;
2. Vision and mission: Why we live;
3. Work: The value of trying;
4. Honesty: The big difference;
5. Service: The magic of being useful; and
6. Education: The virtue of learning.

Alex Dey
www.alexdeyonline.com

In *El Despertador ¡Cómo tener un buen día, todo el día, Todos Los Días!* (The alarm clock, how to have a good day, all day, every day) Mr. Dey shares two very important observations:

> *¿Por qué cuando el exito está disponible para todos, tan pocas personas la aprovechan?*
>
> *El fracaso no existe, solo son experencias en las que se aprende cómo no se hacen las cosas* (Dey 2006, 58).

The first quote asks why is it that when so many people have success within reach, so few people take advantage of it. The second quote affirms that failure does not exist; it is only an experience in which one learns how not to do certain things.

Cesar Lozano
www.cesarlozano.com

In *¿Fracasado yo? ¡Nunco!* (which translates to: Me a failure? Never)
Dr. Lozano offers guidance, suggesting we not succumb to any form of disappointment. And if/or when this setback occurs, know how to handle it.
Here is the advice found on his Web site:

1. *Tenemos el derecho a fallar, a cometer errors. Eso es de humanos.
    Trata de cerrar pronto la herida y estarás bien.*

2. *Si no puedes luchar contra el sentir que has fracasado, ¡no hagas
    un drama! Recurre a alguien que te ayude: en la familia, en los
    amigos o en profesionales del desarrolo humano, y seurgamente
    saldrás del hoyo y versa cómo todo eso que te afectaba simple-
    mente pasará* (Lozano 2010).

The above two quotes translate to:

1. We have the right to fail and commit errors. This is being human.
    Try to heal the problem quickly and you will be fine.

2. If you cannot fight against the failing sensation, do not create any
    drama. Resort to someone that may guide/help you such as a fam-
    ily member, friend, or human resources professional, and surely
    you will come out knowing that what occurred to you was tempo-
    rary and will go away.

Who versus Why

According to Marcus Buckingham, career success guru, "In the end,
the 'what' always trumps the 'why' and the 'who'" (Buckingham 2008, 63).
That is very important when intermingling with Spanish-speakers. If librarians are to succeed in rendering their services to Spanish-speakers, they need
to be conscious of the why, when, how, and who. Here we cover the "what
to say" approach, as many libraries find themselves at a loss with subjects
that are of interest to the Spanish-speaking community. By focusing more
on our profession's strengths instead of its shortcomings, we will be better
positioned. What you say can have a dramatic impact and demonstrate to
the community that you are sincerely interested in their success whether
they are a community member, parent, or educator. A prime example of
how beliefs about "who" are better than beliefs about "why" or "how" is
seen in the results of the 2011 *Library Journal* Paralibrarian of the Year

award, sponsored by DEMCO. Gilda Ramos, a full-time employee at the Patchogue-Medford Library in New York was selected for her efforts as she "delivers and exemplifies phenomenal library service in that role" and by also "combining extraordinary daily contributions to the people of the community with her total belief in the importance of serving others."

When speaking with first-generation parents, ask them why they made the journey to the United States. Chances are that they will respond with "for a better quality of life"—hands down, that is the most common response. But if you pursue the dialogue a little farther, ask them what makes a good city good. Pay attention to their responses—you may gain some ideas of how to better serve them. They may say that they want their children to be successful or have better opportunities. Well, what are better opportunities? At this point they will elaborate what it is they forecast for their children. A very popular response is for their children to obtain a college degree. This is the point where the librarian has an opportunity to influence the Latino parent's knowledge and understanding of how the library may contribute to their overall success. In this case they share what resources are readily available to them while having a conversation about the importance of an education. By speaking freely, the Latino parent will gather that the librarian truly understands and is on the same page as them. Also, inquire as to how they feel living in this new society. Once again, listen carefully to their response. You will learn something, even if they state the obvious. But what is not obvious? Here, your captive Spanish-speaking audience can weigh in on what constitutes a good city, a city that will help them experience the American Dream.

How do you empower and challenge parents? Share information about your community with them that they might not know yet. For example, the number of people with college degrees, how much the local school system spends per pupil, number of teachers per pupil, number of criminal offenses, availability of cultural attractions, number of early childhood education programs, economic development, and health care resources for all ages.

At the same time, keep in mind that these same people are being influenced by such personalities as El Piolin de la Mañana, El Cucuy, and Don Francisco from *Sábado Gigante*. The first two characters are very risqué types and show their affection toward their community through sarcasm and sexual remarks. Wildly popular, they have a wide listener base and great status in the Latino community. Don Francisco, on the other hand, is a famous mainstream TV personality who has entered the lives of many Latino households. He could be compared to Bob Barker of *The Price is Right*.

When discussing Latino teens with their parents, keep in mind that parents like to be informed of their teens' whereabouts and involvement. Teens have had a short tenure in life and have not experienced the many struggles that adults have gone through. That is why parents as well as librarians need to play a bigger role, whether or not teens want to hear your message. When they grow up and reflect on those individuals that made an impact, it is the constant and repetitive proclamations that they recall.

The current population growth of Latino teens has some momentous implications. Two trends Senior Researcher Richard Fry (2009) comments on are:

- Young Latino adults in the United States are more likely to be in school or in the work force now than their counterparts were in previous generations [as previous generations of teens stayed at home more]; and

- The increase in their attachment to school or the work world (which includes employment by the military) has been driven mainly by the changes in the endeavors of young Hispanic females.

High-Achieving Females

Consider the following high-achieving women, who are great role models for female Latina teens. The brief annotations are courtesy of a well-used library database titled Biography in Context.

Hilda L. Solis—Hilda Solis was the choice of President Barack Obama to be his labor secretary.

Janet L. Delgado, Ph.D., M.S.—Jane L. Delgado, Ph.D., is the President and Chief Executive Officer of the National Alliance for Hispanic Health.

Marisol Becerra—Marisol Becerra, 18, an activist with Chicago's Little Village Environmental Justice Organization (LVEJO).

Sonia Sotomayor—Sonia Sotomayor became the first Hispanic-American woman to be nominated to a seat on the U.S. Supreme Court, on May 26, 2009.

Nydia M. Velázquez—Nydia Margarita Velázquez is the first Puerto Rican woman to be elected to the U.S. House of Representatives.

Frances Garcia—Garcia became the first Hispanic woman mayor in the Midwest.

Nancy Sutley—Nancy Sutley was named chairperson of the White House Council on Environmental Quality in December of 2008.

When dealing with the parents of Latino teens, consider yourself a motivational leader and success catalyst. As a librarian, you are keenly positioned to relay such valuable information as you have the collections to support and promote such subject matter. The beauty of this approach is that it affects all areas of life—parenting, employment, education, and relationships, to name a few. The parents in turn will be grateful that someone is taking a vested interest in developing their skills and talents.

Librarians as Forward Thinkers

Latino parents want nothing more than to have a sense that their family will in some way, shape, or form, thrive in today's society. You are in an ideal position to help them acquire that sense—through library services, programs, and materials. When giving reading suggestions or presenting workshops, offer an assortment of American and Latino authors. You can also disclose biographical details about Latino authors that will resonate with your audience.

Forward-thinking, first-generation, Spanish-speaking adults and a majority of second-generation Latino parents are on the same wavelength. They are interested in bettering themselves to ensure that they provide their families with guidance and direction. Some of this acquired knowledge may be in Spanish. At the same time, these same individuals are interested in English literature that will steer them toward success. Every day more books are written on the subject of leadership and achieving the American Dream. In these books you will find information to share with the parents of Latino teens that they will find rewarding and enlightening. One such book is *Obstacles Welcome* (Thomas Nelson 2009) by Ralph de la Vega. Ralph de la Vega came to the United States from Cuba alone at the age of 10, and is now CEO of AT&T's Mobility and Consumer Markets. His book talks about his formula for success.

In *Powerhouse Principles* (Celebra 2008), Jorge Peréz, a wealthy Florida real estate mogul, divulges the principles of his success. In *10-10-10* (Scribner 2009), Suzy Welch provides strategies for making difficult decisions look and feel easy. Her method facilitates the process by clarifying how a particular consequence turns out in 10 minutes, 10 months, and 10 years. When interacting with Latino parents apply these pointers to their own situations. For example, applying Suzy Welch's philosophy, you might ask: How do you, as a parent, benefit in 10 minutes, 10 months, or 10 years from visiting your local public library? Educationally speaking, how do you, as a parent benefit—in 10 minutes, 10 months, or 10 years—from visiting or touring your local institution of higher education once a month? These types of questions prompt dialogue that can assist them in their judgment- and decision-making skills.

To take it a step farther, consider the following quote from an article titled "Rethinking Legalization" from the February 2010 edition of Poder Enterprises Magazine as it relates to illegal immigration: "a new study counters the arguments of fiscal conservatives worried about the costs associated with [immigration] reform. The study . . . suggests legalizing undocumented immigrants would yield $1.5 trillion to the gross domestic product, as well as create additional tax revenue and consumer spending. Besides providing enough capital to pay for the health reform bill, the research found, legalization historically raises wages of all workers" (Poder Enterprises 2010).

Conclusion

There are many lessons that are either new or duplicate. Every conceivable effort was made to bring light to relevant and responsive library services to Latino teens. The complex part is that Latino teens are a moving target. No one brushstroke approach may be used. Instead, careful awareness, understanding, appreciation, and persistent dedication are needed to stay on top of this "now" segment.

One thing is for sure: past services and programs are no longer indicative of future services and programs. These are new times with new and different opportunities and challenges that require change. The negative gaps continue to rise to record highs in many fronts; the paradigm shifts of demographics are ever evolving; and Latino teens are influencing the mainstream as trendsetters and trailblazers when it comes to popular culture. Becoming familiar and most importantly agreeing with these tendencies is something that the library profession needs to embrace in order to captivate Latino teens. After reading *Serving Latino Teens* library staff members must use this information, which must be preceded or accompanied by the implementation of effective and efficient services and programs.

In mid-2011, my brother Ricardo introduced me to a popular phenomenon that landed on YouTube. The video draws attention to Julio Cesar, a waiter turned homeless due to his alcoholism. This individual created the instant sensation motivation phrase "*fua*." In Cesar's own words, "*fua*" is to:

- *tener carácter* (to have character);
- *dar el extra* (to give it all you got); and
- *ser fuerte* (to be strong).

Guess what? Librarians have *fua*! Librarians have character to render services and programs. Librarians do give their all to render services to key constituents. Librarians are strong and dedicated in their efforts to ensure that current and future patrons find what they need or want. This is the art of *fua*, library style. You can also gain much *fua* by reading the complete Libraries Unlimited Professional Guides for Young Adult Librarian Series.

The future of librarianship looks bright. The profession's talent pool is very promising. Our patron base will be there, but they may be expecting innovation and more eServices and ePrograms. Let's stand tall and proud so that today's teens have a successful future. Thank you for caring and for reading this book. Enjoy the journey!

References

Avila, Salvador. 2008. *Crash course in serving Spanish-speakers.* Westport, CT: Libraries Unlimited.

Berry III, John N. 2011. Gilda Ramos. (Cover Story). *Library Journal* 136.4: 30. *MasterFILE Premier* [accessed March 15, 2012].

Biography in Context [database]. Gale Cengage Learning [accessed March 15, 2012].

Buckingham, Marcus. 2008. *The truth about you.* Nashville: Thomas Nelson.

Cesar, Julio [video]. http://www.youtube.com/watch?v=9FrUHfrvlgg& feature=related [accessed March 15, 2012].

Collins, Jim. 2001. *Good to great.* New York: HarperCollins.

Cornejo, Miguel Angel. 1995. *Únete a la excelencia.* México, D.F.: Editorial Grad.

Cruz, Camilo. 2003. *Los genios no nacen ¡se hacen! Cómo programar tu mente para triunfar y ser feliz.* México, D.F.: Editorial Planeta.

Dey, Alex. 2006. *El Despertador ¡Cómo tener un buen día, todo el día, Todos Los Días!* Aimee Spanish Books Publisher.

Fry, Richard. 2009. The *changing pathways of Hispanic youths into adulthood.* Washington, D.C.: Pew Hispanic Center.

Lozano, Cesar. 2010. *¿Fracasado yo? ¡Nunco!* www.cesarlozano.com [accessed March 15, 2012].

El mexicano lee poco, no va a museos y ve mucha tv! 2010. *El Universal*, December 17, http://www.eluniversal.com.mx/cultura/64416.html [accessed March 15, 2012].

Pérez, Jorge. *Powerhouse Principles*. 2009. Tennessee: Celebra Trade.

Rethinking Legalization. 2010. *Poder Enterprise Magazine*, February, 16.

"Rethinking Legalization." February 2010. *Poder Enterprise Magazine*. Page 16 (1).

Welch, Suzy. 2009. *10-10-10*. New York: Scribner.

Appendix A

The following are exemplary programs taking place from coast to coast. Some are library sponsored, while others are run by nonprofit groups but may be easily replicated by libraries.

Latino Youth Leadership Conference

Las Vegas Latin Chamber of Commerce
http://www.lvlcc.com [accessed March 15, 2012]

The Conference

The Latino Youth Leadership Conference was developed through the Education Committee of the Latin Chamber of Commerce 16 years ago to increase the number of Hispanic students attending college while increasing their leadership skills and decreasing the high school dropout rate.

Once a three-day conference, by students' demand it is now a six-day conference held at the University of Nevada, Las Vegas; College of Southern Nevada; and Nevada State College Campuses. Students spend the night at the university dorms to have a better feel for college life.

Totally Outstanding Teen Advocates for the Library (T.O.T.A.L.)

Nashville Public Library
Description by Elyse Adler

Teens need to be heard, be accountable, and be offered leadership skills, a voice, and the responsibility to help create and provide opportunities for themselves and others. T.O.T.A.L. (Totally Outstanding Teen Advocates for the Library) is a group of high school students employed by the Nashville Public Library to work in a shared leadership capacity. They advocate for the library among their peers and the community at large and research, develop, and implement programs for the public. They represent the library at community events, assist in recruiting teen volunteers, and are trained in areas such as leadership skills, team-building, project planning, time management, conflict resolution, and public speaking to sharpen their professional skills and bolster their confidence. T.O.T.A.L. teens also sit on various systemwide committees, and a T.O.T.A.L. teen participated in our Strategic Conversation, a market research and strategic planning initiative that helped the library plan for the future using input from key business and civic leaders as well as the general public. The staff works 12 hours per week after school or on weekends under the direction of a program coordinator and has their own office at the Main Library. Adopting the premise that no one communicates with teens better than other teens, T.O.T.A.L.'s primary goal is to attract a hard-to-reach teen audience to the library by planning and implementing programs and events that appeal to this group with ideas and concepts that matter most to them. With a mission that states *To assist the Nashville Public Library in reaching out to the teen community to promote literacy and to provide positive activities in a safe environment*, T.OT.A.L. also serves the mission of the city's administration and the importance it has placed on youth in our community. As the 2007 winner of the distinguished national Highsmith Award, T.O.T.A.L. has succeeded in making a large impact, both in the broader community as well as on the culture of the Nashville Public Library. Since T.O.T.A.L. staff have been in place, the audience at programs, teen card registration, and circulation of teen materials have all increased. This staff has also helped the library by developing relationships and partnering with other agencies throughout the city. In this capacity, they not only work with youth, but also help bridge gaps by working with young children and adults. We all know that today's youth are our future and that attention needs to be paid to how we serve them. T.O.T.A.L. staff are in a unique position to develop as leaders and then to use those skills to promote the library and provide the highest quality of services and programs both inside and outside our library walls.

A Teen Zone on the Famous Las Vegas Strip

Las Vegas–Clark County Library District
Description by Lauren Campbell

The Teen Zone at the Enterprise Library, a branch of the Las Vegas–Clark County Library District (NV), sits on a corner in the west side of the building behind the reference desk and the magazine shelves. Originally meant as a special collections room that was later converted to house the reference collection, it is separated from the main floor of the library by interior windows, and today it is exactly what the name describes: an area for teen patrons, loosely kids ages 12–17, to find materials specifically geared toward their interests and needs. Large foam purple letters above the windows label it as "Teen Zone," which makes it easy to point out to patrons wondering where YA books are located.

Inside patrons can find YA fiction, high interest nonfiction, graphic novels, comic books, teen magazines, DVDs, and program advertisements. Four orange cushioned lounge chairs are also arranged around end tables, which, after a typical day, are littered with the magazines and Manga teens have read throughout the day. The orange chairs were a conscious choice. Since the color scheme of the rest of the branch is purple we wanted different colored lounge chairs in the Teen Zone to further delineate it as a separate and special place. Collegiate pennants and T-shirts and other memorabilia from schools of higher education as well as inspirational quotes decorate the Teen Zone.

Just outside the entrance to the Teen Zone sit two wire racks. One is dedicated to middle and high school reading lists, the other to classics. The school reading list collection was developed in cooperation with students, nearby teachers, the Young People's Library Department, and the reference department: teachers submitted lists of books they teach, and we made sure we owned or ordered them! Many books on the list are older titles that the district may not own many copies of but that students need yearly. Now these titles are easily assessable to students, and given that all of our paperbacks are not cataloged, they cannot be requested by patrons from other branches, and stay in our library for local students. The classics section goes hand in hand with the reading lists section since many classics are also required reading for high school students. Although all of the books in this section also have copies cataloged and filed with fiction, this is an easy "one stop" section for teens. All books in the classics section are paperback, uncataloged, and have multiple copies so students can (almost) always walk out of the library with the book they came looking for.

Anyone can enter the Teen Zone and actively look for items (after all, as many adults as teens read *Twilight*) but only teens can hang out there for an extended amount of time. And hang out they do. In fact, this area has been so successful as a place for teens to gather or read that we are expanding the Teen Zone to include the larger room immediately next door as well. This will give the teens two adjacent although separate rooms. One will house the main YA collection with comfy chairs for quiet reading, while the other will be dedicated to study tables, games, and more social interaction.

After meeting with several teen patrons at a Teen Advisory Group (TAG) and hearing their concerns and opinions, we are also trying to develop a teen CD section containing popular titles, possibly adding listening stations and rethinking the wall colors. One missing element of the Teen Zone is the lack of computers and other technologies. The one unanimous vote by the TAG group was to add teen-only computers that would allow teens to access MySpace and Facebook. Currently, our children's computers filter those sites as budget constraints will unfortunately not allow us to add technology.

Of course many libraries have more extensive, technologically savvy Teen Zones that have been liberally funded and spent years in the planning stages. We had limited resources and no budget, but Enterprise Library staff had a strong desire to make our Teen Zone a priority, and so we looked around at what we had readily available to made it work.

Enterprise Library Teen Zone

Teen Card Design Contest

Pierce County Library System [Tacoma, Washington]

Description by Judy T. Nelson

As a library system with limited resources and a fairly new deliberate focus on service to teens, we launched a Teen Library Card Contest in the spring of 2009 inviting any teen within our service area to submit their idea for a new library card. It would be offered in the fall of 2009 and available to anyone who wanted it. The card would sport the winning design on one side and have the artist's name on the other along with bar code and other pertinent library information. We wanted teens to be personally connected to the library through the way they accessed the myriad services we provide them. We believed that if teens got a library card that was designed by a fellow teen they would be more likely to try us out. We also believed that once they tried us we would become a place to visit and use. Teens would discover and then use all the homework tools we offer and connect with all the other cool stuff we have as well.

For the past two years the Pierce County Library System has held a systemwide library card campaign to promote library services and increase the number of active card holders in our community. In the Youth Services department we have used this initiative to target eighth and ninth graders in the thirteen school districts we serve. We wanted to deliberately promote the specific tools we provide for student success, especially the ones needing a library card such as the online homework help and other electronic resources and databases.

Since we are new to developing services for teens and have limited dollars and staff we went back to something that has been successful. Along with the Pierce County Library Foundation and several longstanding community partners we have hosted a successful teen poetry and short story writing contest for thirteen years. We added a manga drawing contest to this effort four years ago. We know teens in our county enjoy competing and sharing their talents because of the numbers of unduplicated submissions we get each year. We decided that an effective teen-centered way to promote our card drive school visits would be to make it personal and add the competition aspect to our upcoming card drive. As a library system we don't offer new card designs very often so this would be a unique opportunity. It also fit very nicely into our system marketing strategy, and we decided that anyone who wanted one could get this special teen-designed card.

Because of the writing and drawing contests we have a well-established network of contacts. We target the school districts, their newsletters, art teachers, etc. We also have a MySpace page for the library's teens and all the normal media channels used by our communications department. Since we have partnerships with many of the news media outlets for other large library initiatives, such as Pierce County READS, we were able to leverage their dissemination processes as well. Individual branch locations did guerrilla marketing in their own communities, with flyers, library white boards, and direct community contacts.

We ran the contest in late spring as the annual writing contest was ending. Teens and schools were paying attention to what we were doing because they were watching for the writing winners to be announced and honored. We took that opportunity to hold this additional contest. The timing was also done so that when the librarians visited schools to promote summer reading they were also promoting the final voting on the card designs, which were posted on our Web site.

It turns out that this was a relatively easy project to execute. We have a long successful history of offering the writing and drawing contests to teens. This provided us with a wealth of knowledge about how to execute the actual contest: process, rules, judging, etc. Timing turned out to be the most important thing. We wanted to be able to offer the finished card during our annual fall card drive. With that as an end date, we were able to plan backwards to figure out exactly when to run the contest. Since we placed no restrictions on the type of artwork students could submit, the judges had to be very open-minded because the entries were so diverse.

It is too soon to tell whether or not we have been successful regarding increased teen usage of the library and our online services. The card drive is only just now beginning, and the first cards were offered to any age customers including teens beginning October 1, 2009. We do know that for the library, this contest generated increased public awareness and has given us some credibility when we say we are interested and involved directly in the lives of our communities, in this case our teens. We also know it has given us one more way to connect with teens as we promote library services that are relevant specifically to them. We just don't know yet how effective this strategy will be. We serve a county of 534,000 folks over 1,600 square miles. This contest garnered quite a bit of local press coverage when the judges (art teachers and graphic artists from the county) selected the five finalists. For a first effort, we had 110 unduplicated entrants in the contest. When the PCLS Web site posted the work of the five finalists and opened the online voting polls, 1,240 individuals voted for their choice of winning entry. The contest then received additional coverage when the votes were tallied and the winner and winning design were announced.

For our first effort I think teens were receptive to this opportunity; at least 110 of them were. As fall has approached the requests for the actual card have increased at many of our branches. Teens wanted to know when they could switch out their old cards for the new one. We are also getting scattered requests for information about when the "next" card contest will be held, but at this time no definitive decision has been made about that. The inclination of the Youth Services department is to see if this contest can be replicated every other year, with the previous winning card being officially retired after the two-year period, making that card a keepsake.

Were we successful? We don't know yet because we are using it as part of our annual card drive, our annual middle/high school fall visits to promote the use of the library card, and the library's first ever amnesty week when cards may be changed without a fee and accounts can be reactivated with no penalty. We will monitor the number of new cards issued to teens, as well as the number of teen cards reactivated as part of amnesty week and finally the number of the new teen cards actually given out. At this point, we are pleased with the results of the contest and its role in our overall card drive. Whether or not we consider this a complete success will be determined by the numbers we will collect and the enthusiasm we see from teens during the school visits. We do not see this contest as the only way we are reaching out to our teens to use the library, but for now, it is one strategy.

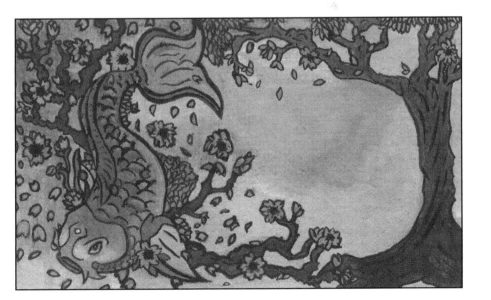

Great Teen Services Start with Staffing

Deschutes Public Library

Description by Sandy Irwin

Libraries are at a turning point in services to teens. Our profession has moved from having a single shelf of YA literature, to playing interactive video games and more. What an exciting time for those who are dedicated to teen services! Yet how many librarians are actually working full-time as a teen services librarian? My guess is that this is rare, especially in small to midsize communities. That's where the Deschutes Public Library makes a difference.

At the time of this article, the Deschutes Public Library has five library branches and an Outreach Services Department, and serves a population of nearly 160,000 residents. Yet we employ three full-time teen services librarians. That's right—three dedicated full-time teen services librarians! Having these three positions has allowed us to have a tangible impact on services to teens, both in our library buildings and throughout the community.

Let's talk about schools. All of us would love to visit schools more often, but how can we fit it in with all of our internal activities? Our teen librarians have created a path into our local schools that not only builds relationships with teens, but also creates more interactions between public librarians and teachers. They do simple acts, such as book talks and pathfinders. They have dedicated book clubs at the school. They bring renowned authors to the schools (Tamora Pierce, Pete Hautman, and Margaret Peterson Haddix, just to name a few). They promote the Teen Summer Reading Program, and get them excited about reading. Most of all, they are able to reach the teens in the place where they spend most of their day—school!

Their school visits translate into library visits. After hearing a great book talk, they are literally running into our buildings and seeking that great book they just heard about. When there, they have access to a librarian who is trained to serve them—they know the collections, have patience when answering questions, and are enthusiastic about serving teens. They learn about the teens' interests and create programs that excite and engage them. The teens become dependent on "their librarian" to be there to answer their questions or just to provide a friendly and familiar face.

Our teen librarians also serve as examples to the rest of the staff. They work with the staff in each branch to help them understand how to provide services to teens, sharing information about teen development and behavior and modeling how to handle their boisterous behavior.

The key to a successful teen program is to have librarians who are solely dedicated to teens and can provide them with the excellent level of service they are seeking.

Today's Teens, Tomorrow's Techies (T4)

Brooklyn Public Library

The Urban Libraries Council has nominated this project as a 2010 Top Innovation. Below you will find a brief description of this project from the Brooklyn Public Library Web site.

http://www.brooklynpubliclibrary.org/support/volunteer/t4 [accessed March 26, 2012].

East Orange Public Library

Serving a large population of English-speaking children with Spanish-speaking parents, the library will offer text messaging in Spanish. The library has four Spanish-speaking staffers who will guide the project. For more on this project, see http://www.libraryjournal.com/lj/community/publicservices/855396-276/story.csp [accessed March 26, 2012].

Appendix B
Caló Glossary

How to use this mini Caló glossary: (lm) stands for literal meaning. This is the official usage of the word in Spanish; (em) refers to extended meaning. This is how the word has evolved within the Latino community and is used distinctly from the literal meaning. Each word is then used in an English sentence so that it is easily understood by non-Spanish-speaking readers.

Agasajar—(lm) to treat with attention and warmth. (em) French kiss. That couple is really *agasajando*—those are deep, sloppy kisses!

Aguitado—(lm) from *agüitarse*, which means to be sad. After he lost his job he became really *aguitado*.

Aranado—no (lm). The (em) is to be married. At the age of 44 *se arano*. At the age of 44 he settles down.

Bironga—no (lm). The (em) refers to an alcoholic drink. There was plenty of *bironga* for the adults to drink at her quinceñera.

Bofió—no (lm). The (em) implies someone that is tired. After 15 minutes of playing soccer he was *bofiado*.

Cábula—no (lm). The (em) entails gossiping. What they were saying about you is pure *cábula*.

Calcos—no (lm). The (em) refers to pants. I bought these Dickies *calcos* at Walmart.

Cantón—no (lm). The (em) denotes a home. I will be buying a *cantón* with five bedrooms once I have saved enough for a down payment.

Clecha—no (lm). The (em) implies a school. Make sure that he goes to *clecha* today because his teachers will notice if he is absent.

Cuetear—no (lm). The (em) suggest to shoot at someone. The city has been witnessing many new *cuetasos* by unknown gunmen.

De aquellas—no (lm). The (em) means fine or excellent. What do you think of my ride? It is *de aquellas*; I wish I had one like it.

Escamado—no (lm). The (em) is someone that is frightened. Don't be that *escamado*—we will back you up.

Ese—no (lm). The (em) is homeboy. Homeboys like to call each other *ese*.

Feria—(lm) is a fair. The (em) is money. Before we go on vacation, let me save up some *feria*.

Gacho—(lm) is bowed or drooping. The (em) is rude, crude, or vulgar. When he drinks too much he is *gacho* toward passing women.

Gafas—(lm) is glasses. The (em) is shades. I purchased my *gafas* at the swap meet to protect my eyes from the summer sun.

Jaina—no (lm). The (em) is girlfriend. I'm taking my *jaina* out on a date tonight to show her my favorite restaurant.

Jando—no (lm). The (em) is hat. Wear your *jando* to protect your face and head—it's going to get over 100 degrees.

Jura—(lm) is to swear to a set obligation. The (em) signifies police. The *jura* let us go. We just looked like the suspects.

Lira—(lm) is a musical instrument made up of ten strings. The (em) is a guitar. I purchased my *lira* from his grandfather, who will give me lessons on playing it.

Orale—no (lm). The (em) is agreement or exclamation. *Orale* homeboy. Where have you been all this time?

Pachanga—no (lm). The (em) is a party or social gathering. You will be invited to my birthday *pachanga*.

Palo—(lm) is a stick. The (em) is to have sexual intercourse. When I get home I'm going to take the wife into the bedroom to try to have me a *palo*.

Pañar—no (lm). The (em) is to purchase. You mom said to *pañar* milk at the store, not beer.

Parro—no (lm). The (em) is to do a favor for someone. Do me a *parro* by loaning me some cash.

Pinta—(lm) is to paint. The (em) is prison. That last thing I want is to be locked up in the *pinta*.

Pisto—no (lm). The (em) is an alcoholic beverage. Homeboy bought the cheapest *pisto* he could find for his drinking buddies.

Rajar—(lm) is to slice. The (em) is to surrender or give up. That boxer didn't *rajar*; he fought on until his opponent was knocked out.

Rallar—(lm) is to grate. The (em) is to get lucky. If you play the casino slots, chances are that you are not going to *rallar* and win anything.

Ranfla—no (lm). The (em) is a vehicle. I have the cleanest *ranfla* in town because I go to the car wash every day.

Refinar—(lm) is to refine. The (em) is to eat. I enjoy going to his pad to *refinar*. His mom makes some killer tamales.

Rola—no (lm). The (em) is a song. Put some oldie *rolas* on the jukebox.

Sariado—no (lm). The (em) is sorry or despicable. The artwork from that dude was *sariado*; my three-year-old cousin does better drawings.

Simon—no (lm). The (em) is yes or to agree. Want to meet up with some high school friends? ¡*Simon!*

Tango—(lm) is tango. The (em) is town. What *tango* were you born in?

Toilido—no (lm). The (em) is toilet. There were no *toilidos* in the desert, so I went behind a bush to relieve myself.

Torcer—(lm) is to bend. The (em) is to be busted or captured. That is his third strike *torcida*; with the stolen goods right in his hands, he's going straight to jail.

Tramos—no (lm). The (em) are pants. Some people purchase their Dickies *tramos* at Walmart.

Tripiada—no (lm). The (em) is to trip out. It was a *tripiado* to know that he was a she.

Trompos—(lm) a spinning top. The (em) is a fight. There were *trompos* every day of the week, as the guys settled disputes with their fists.

Trucha—(lm) is to trout. The (em) is to be cautious or careful. You have to be *trucha* with those credit card companies; sometimes they raise interest rates without telling you.

Túrica—no (lm). The (em) is a casual conversation. Go ahead and have some *túrica* with that girl, see if you can pick her up.

Vato—no (lm). The (em) is dude or fellow friend/homeboy. That *vato* I went to school with goes to college and wants to become a teacher.

Appendix C
Web sites

The following annotations are derived from each individual Web site. All sites were accessed on March 13, 2012.

9500 Liberty

http://www.9500liberty.com

Prince William County, Virginia, becomes ground zero in America's explosive battle over immigration policy when elected officials adopt a law requiring police officers to question anyone they have "probable cause" to suspect is an undocumented immigrant.

Lá Teen

http://www.lateen.com/

English language magazine for teens that addresses culture, sports, fashion, poetry, entertainment, and education.

Revista Tú

http://www.esmas.com/revistatu/

Spanish-language publication from one of Mexico's premier media outlets, Editorial Televisa, that focuses on contemporary issues such as news, fashion, health, and horoscopes.

Latinitas

http://www.latinitasmagazine.org/

    Latinitas is a nonprofit organization that enables young Latinas to achieve personal and academic success through media and technology outreach, thereby addressing the critical state of Latina girls today. While Latina girls ages 12 to 17 are the largest group of minority girls in the country, they are more likely than their non-Hispanic peers to face the four most serious threats to achieving success: depression, pregnancy, substance abuse, and becoming a high school dropout. The solution lies in empowering these young Latinas, strengthening their confidence and expanding their opportunities. With a variety of enriching experiences, Latinitas discover their voices and develop media skills while building solid foundations for their futures.

Vivir Latino

http://vivirlatino.com/

    VivirLatino is a daily publication, featuring news, analysis, and opinions about Latino politics and culture created for the diverse and influential Latino and Latina community in the United States by Latinas.

Música en Español

http://new.e1.music.yahoo.com/

    Everything about Latino music from a Yahoo platform.

Latino MySpace

http://latino.myspace.com/

    A MySpace site for Latinos that showcases people, music, videos, games, and events in both English and Spanish.

Barrio 305

http://www.barrio305.com/

    Cellular wallpaper for cell phones powered by Android.

Batanga

http://www.batanga.com/es/

Batanga offers music, entertainment, local and community news, and top videos in both English and Spanish.

Cyloop

http://www.cyloop.com/

Cyloop is a social music application that allows users to create a powerful and personalized multimedia experience with one of the most extensive audio and video libraries on the web. On Cyloop you can listen to and collect millions of songs, from the world's leading artists to local independent acts, and follow all the activity surrounding your favorite artists in a truly personalized manner.

Mun²

http://holamun2.com/

Mun2 is part of Telemundo cable, the cable division of the Telemundo network. Telemundo, the Spanish-language network dedicated to developing original programming for the U.S. hispanic market, is owned by NBC Universal, a division of General Electric.

MyGrito

http://www.mygrito.com/

MyGrito is a place to shout out what you're doing right now. Going to a party with your amigos? Hechale un grito a tus friends. Just launched a new Web site? Give your clients a shout-out. Thinking of going to a movie? Want a recommendation? Send a question shout-out. MyGrito is micro-blogging with a Latino twist.

Terra

http://www.terra.com/

Terra is a site for news, sports, entertainment, lifestyle, music, and chat in both English and Spanish.

Tiki Tiki

http://tikitikiblog.com/

The Tiki Tiki is a warm, fun, familial space where we can share stories, videos, photographs, and links of interest to Latinas and Latinos—from the first generation to the third and beyond. You will see yourself here because, like you, we were born into families who know what an ñ sounds like and that all good parties, no matter the size, require pushing back the furniture to dance the evening away.

Vostu

http://www.vostu.com/

Vostu is the largest social game developer serving the Brazilian market with more than 20 million active users across all of our games on Orkut. From farm-building games to café-management, to soccer role-playing games, our vision is simple: to bring you closer to your friends and family through our fun and exciting games.

Perez Hilton

http://perezhilton.com/

Perez was named the #1 Web Celeb for 2007, 2008, and 2009 by *Forbes Magazine* and has recently been tapped as one of the 15 most influential Hispanics in the US by *People in Español* and named 2009 Hispanic of the Year by Hispanic Magazine. Since launching in 2004, PerezHilton .com—originally named PageSixSixSix.com—has become one of the leading go-to sites for celebrity news, garnering over 300 million hits a month.

Teen Health and Wellness

http://www.teenhealthandwellness.com/

Teen Health & Wellness: Real Life, Real Answers—the award-winning, critically acclaimed online resource—provides middle and high school students with nonjudgmental, straightforward, standards-aligned, curricular and self-help support. Topics include diseases, drugs, alcohol, nutrition, mental health, suicide, bullying, green living, financial literacy, and more. Developed for teens, with their unique concerns and perspective, Teen Health & Wellness draws on Rosen's award-winning series, including *Coping*, *Need to Know*, and others. Thoroughly updated and revised for online use, all content is reviewed by leading professionals in medicine, mental health, nutrition, guidance, and career counseling

All My Faves

http://www.allmyfaves.com/

AllMyFaves is the ultimate home page, offering an innovative visual exploration of the Internet.

Appendix D
Graphic Novels in Spanish

Astro Boy by Osamu Tezuka. Pujol & Amado S.L.L, 2003.

A visionary Tezuka shows us a paranormal view of the world of robots from the 1950s, which is, curiously, set in 2003. In this work the author shows his simple view of what he thought the 21st century would be like.

Black Jack by Osamu Tezuka. Desnivel, 1998.

A skillful surgeon who acts outside the legal circuit because he does not like the paperwork or the hierarchy. He charges his wealthy patients too much but treats his poor patients for free. The author relates the importance of life and how medical attention is not the same for different societies.

Bleach by Tite Kubo. No publisher listed. 2006.

Bleach follows the adventures of Ichigo Kurosaki after he accidentally obtains the power of a *shinigami*, a Japanese death personification similar to the Grim Reaper, from Rukia Kuchiki. Gaining these abilities forces him to take on the duties of defending humans from evil spirits and guiding departed souls to the afterlife. Part of Japan's favorite 10 series, this manga has sold over 50 million copies and has been a best seller in the United States as well.

Capitan Tusbasa by Yoichi Takahashi. No Publisher listed. 2007.

On the streets of Tsubasa, a soccer ball is respected like it is in Argentina or Brazil or even a championship. Experience the loneliness of the goal keeper, the critical decisions of the offense, and the sacrifice of the defense. Soccer will never be the same again.

Captain Harlock by Leiji Matsumoto. Pujol & Amado S.L.L., 2003.

Captain Harlock is banished from Earth and becomes a Space Pirate who plunders the known universe.

Cardcaptor Sakura by Clamp. Editorial LVREA, 2001.

The young Sakura fights against the evil forces to recover the lost cards of Clow in one of the most popular manga titles.

Claymore by Norihiro Yagi. No Publisher listed. 2007.

The Claymores are female warriors that are half human, half demon. They answer the call for help of innocent villagers who are attacked by cannibalistic monsters called The Yomas. The warriors fight against them with big swords and try to prevent the extinction of humanity. Follow Claire, one of the Claymores, in her adventures in this popular manga.

D Gray-Man by Hoshino Katsura. IVREA, 2010.

Allen Walker, a member of a secret organization within the English Victorian Reserves that works for the Vatican, has been called to active duty to search and destroy Akumas. These entities are demons that take over human bodies and start problems wherever they go.

Death Note by Tsugumi Ohba. Viz Media L.C.C., 2007.

Death Note has come to an end; its twelve volumes infiltrated the libraries of Manga Aficionados in the country, meanwhile its legend grows more by word of mouth. *Death Note* is a classic that will be read over and over again. The series centers on Light Yagami, a high school student who discovers a supernatural notebook, the titular "Death Note," dropped on Earth by a *shinigami* (grim reaper) named Ryuk. The Death Note grants its user the ability to kill anyone whose face they have seen by writing the victim's name in the notebook while having a picture of the victim in his mind, since there is the possibility of several people having the same name. The story follows Light's attempt to create and rule a world cleansed of evil using the notebook and the complex conflict between him and his opponents. *Death Note* was nominated for Best Manga at the 2006 American Anime Awards.

Fushigi Yugi: Genbu by Yuu Watase. No Publisher listed. 2007.

Fushigi Yugi: Genbu, the origin of the legend, is a prequel to *Fushigi Yugi: The Mysterious Game*, in which Yuu Watase tells us the story of Takiko Okuda, the first person who opened the book of the universe of the Four Gods.

Fushigi Yugi: Misteriosos by Yuu Watase. Glenat, 2002.

The young girl Miaka travels to a Fantasy Kingdom through a magic book called "The universe of the Four Gods." There she will turn into the guardian of good versus the evil forces that hide in the dark. Passionate adventures of people that live in two worlds: enter the exciting imagination and the tedious reality.

Gentlemen Alliance by Arina Tanemura. No publisher listed. 2007.

Haine left a life of crime and joined the Imperial Academy, where she is currently studying her first year for her bachelors. Her idol is Shizumasa, whom everyone calls "The Emperor" because of his riches, fame, and influence in the school. Haine thinks of nothing else but getting close to him, but it is not easy.

Gintama by Hideaki Sorachi. No Publisher listed. 2007.

The unfortunate landing of the extraterrestrials Amanto in the capital of Japan and the new law banning the samurai to carry weapons is causing a stir. But with all of that, one man maintains his soul of a warrior—his name is Gintoki Sakata. Can this fearless warrior break the corruption into two pieces with his sword?

Inu-Yasha by Rumiko Takahashi. LARP Editores, 2004.

The ingredients of this best seller are adventure, mystery, action, lots of monsters, and a drop of intriguing romance. The series follows a time-traveling high school student, a half demon, a lecherous monk, a fox demon, a demon slayer, and a *nekomata* during the Sengoku period as they seek to find all the fragments of the Jewel of Four Souls and to keep them out of the hands of evildoers, especially Naraku. This manga won the 2002 Shogakukan Manga Award for best shonen title of the year.

Love Hina by Ken Akamatsu. Pujol & Amado S.L.L., 2002.

Keytaro is the only male student in an all-female school, which results in hilarious situations. But a promise between two kids will have consequences now that they are adults.

Naruto by Masashi Kishimoto. Pujol & Amado S.L.L., 2002.

Naruto is an ongoing Japanese manga series written and illustrated by Masashi Kishimoto. The plot tells the story of Naruto Uzumaki, an adolescent ninja who constantly searches for recognition and aspires to become a Hokage, the ninja in his village who is acknowledged as the leader and the strongest of all. Selling over 70 million copies in its native Japan, this series is quickly taking off in countries all over the world.

Negima by Ken Akamatsu. No Publisher listed. 2006.

The magic of Harry Potter and a touch of *Love Hina* give author Ken Akamatsu a hand in this new manga. Negi Springfield is a 10-year-old kid who is going to graduate from Magic School. For his final exam he has to be a professor of English in an all-girl school in Japan, which provokes a lot of problems and adventures.

Ranma ½ by Rumiko Takahashi. Pujol & Amado S.L.L., 2002.

When young Ranma and his father fell into a Chinese warehouse of Zhou Quan Xiang and touched cold water, they were transformed into a panda (father) and a girl. One of the most fun and original works in the history of comics!

Rurouni Kenshin by Nobuhiro Watsuki. Viz, 2008.

Kenshin swore to never kill again, so now he only fights with his dull sword. He intends to leave his criminal past behind him, even though his past seems to follow him. The adventures of this lethal samurai warrior, an assassin in the Japanese middle ages, are the most-read books in Spain, converting this title into a best seller.

Saint Seiya by Masami Kurumada. Pujol & Amado S.L.L., 2003.

Based on the popular series Saint Seiya: The Warriors of the Zodiac, comes Saint Seiya Episode G, a prequel from Masami Kurumada. Situated seven years before the Intergalactic Tournament, Episode G is centered on the Soldiers.

Samurai Deeper Kyo by Kamijyo Akimine. No Publisher listed. 2005.

Samurai, adventures in old-time Japan, a bit of magic, and women? Kyo is a demon trapped in the body of a samurai student in a Japan fuller of magic and battles that you can imagine. An action series with a magnificent focus on mythology, samurai, and Bushido.

Shaman King by Hiroyuki Takei. Viz. 2005.

Manta is an absentminded student in his school. One day he meets Yoh, a mysterious student who not only becomes his friend but also shows him the way of shamanism. Yoh is looking for a chance to be King of the Shamans. *Shaman King* is one of the most popular mangas in Japan and has sold over 16 million copies abroad.

The Prince of Tennis by Takeshi Konomi. No publisher listed. 2006.

A talented kid fights his way onto the high school tennis team. His dark ambition is to seek the destruction of his father, who is a star in that sport. A manga full of suspense and passion.

Trigun by Yasuhiro Nightow. No publisher listed. 2005.

Trigun is a futuristic western with lots of humor. Vash, the main star in this manga, is an inexperienced gun fighter who tends to wreak havoc wherever he goes. To be sure that he does not destroy anything, he travels with two insurance agents, Meryl and Milly, who try to put a stop to Vash's hardheaded ideas.

Yu Yu Hakusho by Yoshihiro Togashi. No Publisher listed. 2005.

Yusuke Urameshi is a street-brawling delinquent with a tough guy approach to everything. Yusuke's mother, Atsuko, an alcoholic, had him at the age of 14 and took a backseat in raising her son. However, no one expects a sudden act of heroism on his part: he dies trying to save a little boy from a speeding car. When he arrives in the afterlife, he is informed that the child would have miraculously survived and had it not been for him the child would have one less scratch on his right arm. Now King Enma, the Judge of Hell, allows him to relive his life as long as he complies. *Yu Yu Hakusho* has sold more than 44,000,000 copies in Japan alone. It won the Shogakukan Manga Award for shonen manga.

Appendix E
Did You Know?

Did you know? is a list of recent accolades by prominent Latinos from all walks of life. This list is just the tip of the iceberg as there are many, many more recent accomplishments in every part of the country.

- **Sonia Sotomayor** became the first Latina/o to be nominated and confirmed to a seat on the U.S. Supreme Court?

- In 1865 Chilean **Phillip Bazaar** became the first Hispanic Medal of Honor winner?

- In 1980 Mexican American bodybuilder **Rachel Elizondo McLish** became the first winner of the U.S. Women's Bodybuilding Championship?

- In 1970 Stanford University football quarterback **Jim Plunkett** became the first Hispanic Heisman Trophy winner?

- **Allison Iraheta** finished fourth on the eighth season of *American Idol?* She signed a record deal.

- During the 2008 Beijing Olympics **Henry Cejudo** won a gold medal in wrestling? He is the youngest American to have won a wrestling gold medal. Both of his parents were undocumented; his mom is now a legal resident.

- **Mayte Michelle Rodriguez** is an actress of Dominican and Puerto Rican descent who is best known for her tough-role acting? She has appeared in several big movies such as *Fast & Furious*, *Blue Crush*, and *S.W.A.T.*

- **Mark Sanchez** was the starting quarterback for the New York Jets during the 2009 season? As a rookie he was prominent in leading the Jets to the championship round. Sanchez is a third-generation Mexican American from Southern California who attended the University of Southern California.

- Guatemalan immigrant Lance Corporal **José Gutierrez** was the first U.S soldier killed in Iraq? He was awarded U.S. citizenship after he was killed.

Index

About the Author

SALVADOR AVILA has been a library ambassador for over 15 years. A native of the Imperial Valley, California, he graduated from the University of Arizona's School of Library and Information Sciences. He has been happily employed with the Las Vegas-Clark County Library District (NV) for the past 15 years in several capacities. Avila is currently the Enterprise Library branch manager. In 2008 he authored *Crash Course in Serving Spanish-Speakers*. He was the recipient of the 2003 Críticas Librarian of the Year award; 2006 Library Journal Mover & Shaker citation; and 2003 Las Vegas Latin Chamber of Commerce Award in Distinction in Culture. He served on the ALA Council, where he and a colleague helped pass a Resolution in Support of Immigrants' Rights and participated in the Urban Libraries Council Executive Leadership Institute. In 2006, he spearheaded the Nevada Spanish Language Outreach Program initiative sponsored by WebJunction and the Nevada State Library and Archives. In 2007–2009, he was a governing body member of Nevada State High School (NSHS). NSHS assists high school students in transitioning to college. He also served on the 2003–2004 ALA Pura Belpré Awards Selection Committee and also taught a course titled Library Skills at the College of Southern Nevada. His favorite fiction book is *Chicano* by Richard Vasquez and favorite nonfiction book is *Good to Great* by Jim Collins.

18935323R00087

Made in the USA
San Bernardino, CA
06 February 2015